Practical Ideas for Teaching Primary Science

CRITICAL
TEACHING

You might also like the following books from Critical Publishing

Teaching Systematic Synthetic Phonics and Early English
By Jonathan Glazzard and Jane Stokoe
978-1-909330-09-2 In print

Primary School Placements: A Critical Guide to Outstanding Teaching
By Catriona Robinson, Branwen Bingle and Colin Howard
978-1-909330-45-0 In print

Teaching and Learning Early Years Mathematics: Subject and Pedagogic Knowledge
By Mary Briggs
978-1-909330-37-5 In print

Beyond Early Reading
By Ed David Waugh and Sally Neaum
978-1-909330-41-2 In print

Inclusive Primary Teaching
By Janet Goepel, Helen Childerhouse and Sheila Sharpe
978-1-909330-29-0 In print

Understanding and Enriching Problem Solving in Primary Mathematics
By Patrick Barmby, David Bolden and Lynn Thompson
978-1-909330-69-6 In print

Most of our titles are also available in a range of electronic formats. To order please go to our website www.criticalpublishing.com or contact our distributor, NBN International, 10 Thornbury Road, Plymouth PL6 7PP, telephone 01752 202301 or email orders@nbninternational.com.

Practical Ideas for Teaching Primary Science

 Vivian Cooke & Colin Howard

CRITICAL
TEACHING

British Library Cataloguing in Publication Data
A CIP record for this book is available from the British Library

ISBN: 978-1-909682-29-0

This book is also available in the following ebook formats:

MOBI ISBN: 978-1-909682-30-6
EPUB ISBN: 978-1-909682-31-3
Adobe e-reader ISBN: 978-1-909682-32-0

The rights of Vivian Cooke and Colin Howard to be identified as the authors of this work have been asserted by them in accordance with the Copyright, Design and Patents Act 1988.

Cover and text design by Greensplash Limited
Project Management by Out of House Publishing
Printed and bound in Great Britain by TJ International

Critical Publishing
152 Chester Road
Northwich
CW8 4AL
www.criticalpublishing.com

Contents

Acknowledgements

We are appreciative of the University of Worcester's support when writing this book and for the support of our colleagues and friends who have inspired us in making this book a reality.

We are grateful to the many tutors, students and pupils who have provided us with the wealth of experience in teaching primary, undergraduate and postgraduate science that has helped inform our writing.

We are extremely indebted to Julia Morris from Critical Publishing whose editorial skills, critical feedback, patience and belief in us have made this book possible.

Finally we would like to thank our immediate families for allowing us the time away from them, in particular Adrian and Angela who have supported us in this journey.

Meet the authors

Vivian Cooke is a senior lecturer in primary science and Acting Head of the Primary Centre within Initial Teacher Education (ITE) at the University of Worcester. She began her teaching career as a primary school teacher with responsibility for science, design and technology and ICT. She has worked in two other higher education institutions as a senior lecturer in science on postgraduate, undergraduate and Masters courses as well as being PGCE course leader for Early Years, primary and two-year PGCE courses.

Colin Howard is a senior lecturer in primary science within ITE at the University of Worcester. He has been involved in primary education for over 24 years, 14 of which have been as a successful head teacher in both small village and large primary school settings. He has been involved in inspecting schools for the Diocese of Hereford as a S48 SIAS Inspector and has a strong research interest in the influence that school buildings have upon their stakeholders.

- talked about the features of their own immediate environment and how environments might vary from one another;

- made observations of animals and plants and explained why some things occurred and talked about changes;

- been developing their scientific skills such as questioning, communicating, measuring and simple problem solving.

The contents and features of the book

Chapters 1 and 2 set the scene by looking at the nature of science and what makes an effective science lesson. Chapters 3 to 11 then cover the statutory topic areas as stated in the new curriculum (DfE, 2013). Each chapter starts with a visual concept map which highlights the key areas to be addressed within the chapter, and there is a section on the common misconceptions and ideas that pupils encounter when studying this content. Suggested key vocabulary is provided to help teachers meet the new curriculum's statutory requirements. Factfiles are included in each subject to help readers secure their own subject knowledge before they go on to help children understand the new topic. The critical questions at the end of each chapter provide an opportunity for critical reflection on the issues discussed in the chapter and a chance for you to develop your future teaching. All chapters include direct links to the new primary curriculum science programme of study, along with useful health and safety notes. Each core chapter also includes suggestions of how the topics covered may be extended through cross-curricular links, and highlights additional reading and web links that may be used to support the study of each focus area.

Chapter 1 provides a discussion of the nature of primary science and why it is important in the twenty-first century. It looks at scientific enquiry and working scientifically. It discusses the need for science skills alongside the development of conceptual knowledge and understanding, and how scientists work. It also looks at the role of talk and the importance of teachers taking account of children's scientific ideas. Readers are asked to reflect on their own teaching and how they synthesise the two aspects of science in their teaching.

Chapter 2 allows the reader to consider what makes an effective science lesson and the different factors that contribute to this such as teaching strategies, planning, the structure of science lessons, meeting the needs of all pupils, carrying out assessments and providing feedback. Readers are asked to reflect on the teaching strategies they use, their subject knowledge and how they meet the diverse needs of their pupils.

Chapter 3 examines the similarities and differences between animals and humans and the factors that are vital for living things to develop, flourish and survive. This chapter will provide teachers with useful subject knowledge and activities covering aspects of life processes such as nutrition and basic physiology.

Chapter 4, Plants, habitats and living things, explores the extensive vocabulary associated with this topic and asks readers to consider different ways in which children can become familiar with and use scientific terminology correctly. It looks at plant classification, structure and life cycle, the life processes of plants and animals and feeding relationships, adaptations and human impact. It demonstrates how the outdoor environment familiar to young children can be effectively used by the teacher to develop scientific knowledge.

Chapter 5, Evolution and inheritance, provides creative ideas for teachers to help children understand how humans and living things have evolved and adapted through time, how the fittest of the species have survived and how, through generations, such changes have made them dominant within their environment.

Chapter 6 looks at children's ideas about everyday materials and their properties, including the classification of materials and how different materials are used in everyday life. It presents activities to help teachers develop children's understanding of mechanical, physical and chemical changes as well as exploring the differences between melting and dissolving.

Chapter 7 on the Earth and space presents very common children's misconceptions on what causes day and night, the seasons and the phases of the Moon. It discusses the shape and scale of the Moon, the Earth, the Sun and the solar system and illustrates how teachers can use models and analogies, including the use of ICT, to make these complex ideas accessible to pupils.

Chapter 8 provides enrichment ideas and teaching strategies relating to rocks and soils, helping you to show pupils the rich variety of rock types that exist. Both natural and man-made materials are considered and how the origins of rocks are found in the geological history of our Earth. It considers the many and varied life forms that have roamed Earth and how a record of their existence can be found in the rocks. Ideas are provided to demonstrate how, over time, a variety of soil types have developed to cover the land on our planet.

Chapter 9 focuses on the sources of light and whether it may be observed from its primary or secondary sources of origin. It helps teachers to teach children to understand how we see light and how natural phenomena such as shadows are created and may be recorded. It provides ideas to encourage children to think about the sources of reflection and how light makes objects visible and adds colour to their world.

Chapter 10 promotes a study of a range of forces from gravity, which keeps us on this world, to resistant forces such as friction, which can be used to slow us down when going too fast. Teaching suggestions enable children to think about the effects such forces have upon their lives and how they can be used to benefit humans. Magnetic forces are also covered in this chapter.

Chapter 11 focuses on teaching the topic of sound. It provides suggestions for teachers to encourage children to think about how sound travels and what controls the loudness and pitch of a sound. It encourages teachers to allow children to consider how the world that they hear is constantly changing as a result of factors that control sounds.

In summary, the book provides a readily accessible resource full of practical teaching strategies and ideas for student teachers and practising teachers that is structured to reflect the key focus areas of study for pupils in primary science, based on the new national curriculum

(DfE, 2013). It also enables teachers and trainees to reflect on their own subject knowledge of science and challenges them to critically evaluate their own teaching of science to become more effective teachers.

References

DfE (2013) *Teachers' Standards*. www.gov.uk/government/uploads/system/uploads/attachment_data/file/208682/Teachers__Standards_2013.pdf (accessed 17 February 2014).

1 The nature of science teaching and working scientifically

Introduction

The Education Reform Act 1988 had a profound effect on the place of science in the primary curriculum in England, Wales and Northern Ireland as, since then, the teaching of science has been statutory and the science that is taught in primary schools is prescribed. This chapter deals with the following important aspects of science.

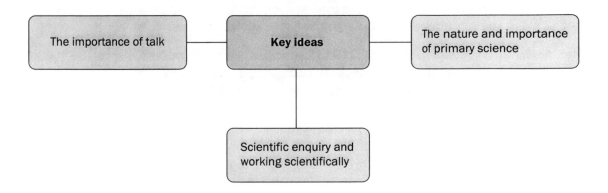

The nature and importance of primary science

Primary science provides children with the skills and knowledge that they need to help them understand the world around them. It helps them to make sense of the changes in our increasingly technological world and prepares them for life in the twenty-first century. Science makes children scientifically literate by enabling them to have a broad understanding of key ideas in science, as well as helping them to apply those ideas to everyday events. It gives pupils the skills to make decisions with confidence about scientific issues that affect us all and understand the implications of science now and in the future. Science can help develop children's curiosity and their sense of wonder and nurture useful attitudes such as perseverance, critical reflection, flexibility in thinking and being sensitive to other points of view. These can be applied to other aspects of their lives.

The new national curriculum (DfE, 2013) describes how science has changed our lives and is vital to the world's future prosperity, and states that all pupils should be taught essential aspects of the knowledge, methods, processes and uses of science. It also describes how science can develop a sense of excitement and curiosity in children about natural phenomena. It describes how the social and economic implications of teaching science are taught most appropriately within the wider school curriculum and how you may wish to use different contexts to maximise pupils' engagement with and motivation to study science. Science can thus effectively be applied and referred to in other curriculum areas such as geography or history, for instance when children are learning about pollution, or how ideas about scientific phenomena have changed over time.

The dual aspect of science

The outcomes of undertaking science activities in your primary classroom will result in children developing conceptual knowledge and understanding about important scientific ideas like ourselves and other living things, materials and their properties, electricity, forces or light. This will require pupils to process information, handle data and use problem-solving skills. These process skills can be defined as the methods and strategies that scientists use to find answers and explanations. They include the ability to ask questions, make predictions, hypothesise, create tests, take measurements, collect data and look for patterns and explanations. This is referred to as the dual aspect of science, where conceptual knowledge and understanding is developed through the application of process skills.

The new national curriculum (DfE, 2013) specifies *working scientifically* as the nature, processes and methods of science that each year group should understand. It states, however, that it should not be taught as a separate strand, but should be embedded within the other programmes of study. The notes and guidance provide examples of how scientific methods and skills might be linked to specific elements of content and advises that children's scientific questions should be answered using a range of different scientific enquiries.

FACTFILE

The AKSIS (ASE-King's Science Investigations in Schools) project identified six different forms of enquiry that can answer scientific questions:

1.   Exploring, for example observing the behaviour of objects or events such as the germination of a seed.

2.   Fair testing, examining the relationship between variables and changing one variable while keeping another variable the same, for example when investigating which substance dissolves best in water.

3. Pattern seeking, for instance making observations and measurements and finding patterns in data (eg do people with long legs jump higher?). The bigger the sample, the more reliable the data.

4. Classifying and identifying, for instance grouping items and objects together based on observation (eg identifying and classifying creatures found in a pond), which encourages pupils to look closely at similarities and differences.

5. Investigating models, for instance simulations of real-life situations such as what causes day and night.

6. Technological enquiry, involving the application of scientific skills, for example designing a burglar alarm where children will apply their understanding of electrical flow.

A wide range of enquiry methods thus need to be used in your primary classroom, and not just fair testing, which has perhaps previously been over-used by teachers. In the Early Years children's enquiries will have centred on exploratory, grouping and sorting activities. As children progress through the primary phase they should be exposed to the full range of different enquiries listed above.

Scientific enquiry and working scientifically

Key Stage 1

In Key Stage 1, the national curriculum (DfE, 2013) describes how pupils should experience and observe phenomena and look closely at the world, asking questions and being curious. It points to the need to develop scientific ideas by pupils using different types of scientific enquiry to answer their questions, including observing changes over time, noticing patterns, grouping and classifying, carrying out simple comparative tests and finding things out using secondary sources of information.

Children need to be able to use scientific language to talk about their findings and communicate their ideas in a variety of ways which may be in verbal or pictorial form, perhaps accompanied by some simple writing. It is important that your pupils learn science through first-hand practical experiences and that they manipulate objects and materials themselves, for example sorting and classifying materials into different groups.

In Years 1 and 2, the new national curriculum states that pupils should be able to:

- *ask simple questions and recognise that they can be answered in different ways;*
- *observe closely, using simple equipment;*
- *perform simple tests;*
- *identify and classify;*

- *use their observations and ideas to suggest answers to questions;*

- *gather and record data to help in answering questions.*

(DfE, 2013, page 147)

It states that these opportunities for working scientifically should be provided across Years 1 and 2 so that the expectations in the programme of study can be met by the end of Year 2. Pupils are not expected to cover each aspect for every area of study.

Encourage your pupils to explore their surroundings and ask their own questions, for example *Which would be the best coat to keep teddy dry, or why do leaves fall off some trees in the autumn?* Remember to use secondary sources of information too, such as books, photographs and videos, to help pupils find the answers to some of their questions. During children's enquires, use attention-focusing questions such as *Did you notice? What is happening?* and encourage the children to measure and count by asking questions such as *How many?* or *How long?* Pupils need to be able to develop the skills to compare items, so ask them questions such as *Is it faster? Is it heavier? Is it lighter?* Encourage their problem-solving skills by asking problem-solving questions, such as *How could you stop the ice cube from melting?* Give children the time to respond to your questions and encourage all of your pupils to participate, perhaps by allowing a short discussion with a partner or a group before providing them with the answers. Be an effective role model by listening carefully to the pupils' responses, probe their answers and build on them and value what the children have to say. If the answer is wrong, try to give constructive feedback or encourage another pupil to help them out.

Children are more likely to engage with science if your science enquiries are set in real-life contexts which are relevant to them, for example, the outdoors. Centres of interest such as a focus table with a collection of resources can be effective in stimulating enquires and encouraging the children to come up with their own questions. Encourage pupils to use as many of their senses as safely as possible and ask them to observe similarities as well as differences as these will allow them to look for patterns and relationships. Provide a range of observational aids such as hand lenses, viewers and microscopes and give support to young pupils when measuring. Children can record their findings in the form of pictures and you can help the less able or those with special needs by being their scribe. Encourage them to talk about what they have done and explain what has happened, using simple scientific language. Taking photographs of the children undertaking their enquiry and recording this in a class book with children's comments is also an effective strategy.

Lower Key Stage 2

In lower Key Stage 2, the new national curriculum (DfE, 2013), describes how children should progress to broadening their scientific view of the world around them by exploring, talking about, testing and developing their ideas and beginning to develop their ideas about functions, relationships and interactions. It notes how pupils should ask their own questions about what they observe and make some decisions about which types of scientific enquiry are likely to be the best ways of answering them, including observing changes over time, noticing patterns, grouping and classifying things, carrying out simple comparative and fair tests and finding things out using secondary sources of information. It encourages pupils first to talk about and then to write about what they have found out using appropriate scientific language. In Years 3 and 4 pupils should be able to use the following practical scientific processes and skills through the teaching of the programme of study content:

- *asking relevant questions and using different types of scientific enquiries to answer them;*
- *setting up simple practical enquiries, comparative and fair tests;*
- *making systematic and careful observations and, where appropriate, taking accurate measurements using standard units, using a range of equipment, including thermometers and data loggers;*
- *gathering, recording, classifying and presenting data in a variety of ways to help in answering questions;*
- *recording findings using simple scientific language, drawings, labelled diagrams, keys, bar charts, and tables;*
- *reporting on findings from enquiries, including oral and written explanations, displays or presentations of results and conclusions;*
- *using results to draw simple conclusions, make predictions for new values, suggest improvements and raise further questions;*
- *identifying differences, similarities or changes related to simple scientific ideas and processes;*
- *using straightforward scientific evidence to answer questions or to support their findings.*

(DfE, 2013, page 155)

Provide pupils with a range of experiences to encourage them to ask their own questions and decide which type of enquiry will best answer that question. Pupils will still need help with formulating their questions. If carrying out a fair test, for example, you will need to support them during the various stages of the enquiry by questioning and prompting, by providing or suggesting the resources and measuring equipment they could use, showing them how to use these accurately using standard units and how to record their results. Give pupils the opportunity to use new equipment, such as thermometers or data loggers to measure changes in temperature. As they get older, pupils will need to decide what data to collect, what observations they will make and the equipment they will use. Pupils may have difficulty when writing about their enquiry so provide writing frames for investigations with headings which distinguish between what they did, how they recorded it, their observations and then an explanation of what happened.

Help children develop their prediction skills when carrying out comparative and fair tests. This important skill encourages pupils to think ahead and focus on the key variables and the relationship between these variables. It will also help them think about what they are going to measure and how, as well as the need to refer to their everyday experiences and scientific knowledge and understanding on which to base their prediction. A useful strategy is to group the children and ask each group to brainstorm what they already know about the topic under discussion. Then ask the children to feedback, record the ideas using the interactive white-board and create a concept map. Children can then refer to this bank of ideas when asked to give a reason for their prediction and thus form a hypothesis.

Pupils need to be able to record their evidence carefully and systematically during any investigation so that they can see patterns and make sense of their results. This is often best done through the use of tables which convey a great deal of information without the need for too much writing. Some children may need guidance on the format of their table and how the data should be organised. A useful thing to do is to check children's tables before they start collecting their data. Ask children to interpret tables of data using questions such as *What does the first column describe?* before considering patterns in data. Another useful strategy to develop children's skills in recording and interpreting data in tables is to provide them with tables of data and ask them to match different descriptions to the different parts of the table. Encourage children to use their mathematical knowledge and understanding when explaining their scientific findings.

Many children have difficulty when describing, explaining and interpreting their results. They can describe and read data presented in a table or simple graph, but are less likely to evaluate that data. They tend to describe patterns rather than explain them. Help the children with this by making a clear distinction between what is an observation and what is an explanation.

Upper Key Stage 2

In upper Key Stage 2, pupils should develop a deeper understanding of a wider range of scientific ideas. The new national curriculum (DfE, 2013) describes how this should be done through exploring and talking about their ideas, asking their own questions and analysing functions, relationships and interactions more systematically. By the top end of Key Stage 2, pupils should encounter more abstract ideas and begin to understand how the world works. It is important for your pupils to realise that scientific explanations are tentative and have changed over time, so provide them with examples, such as our ideas about the Earth and the Solar System or Darwin's evolution of species. Pupils are expected to use different types of enquiry including observing changes over time, noticing patterns, grouping and classifying, carrying out comparative and fair tests and using a wide range of secondary sources of information. Encourage your pupils to draw conclusions based on the data they have collected and use their knowledge and understanding to explain what they have found out. During Years 5 and 6 pupils should be taught to use the following practical scientific methods, processes and skills through the teaching of the programmes of study content:

- *planning different types of scientific enquiries to answer questions, including recognising and controlling variables where necessary;*
- *taking measurements, using a range of scientific equipment, with increasing accuracy and precision, taking repeat readings when appropriate;*
- *recording data and results of increasing complexity using scientific diagrams and labels, classification keys, tables, scatter graphs, bar and line graphs;*

- *using test results to make predictions to set up further comparative and fair tests;*

- *reporting and presenting findings from enquiries, including conclusions, causal relationships and explanations of and a degree of trust in results, in oral and written forms such as displays and other presentations;*

- *identifying scientific evidence that has been used to support or refute ideas or arguments.*

(DfE, 2013, page 166)

Pupils should now be able to make decisions about the observations they make and the measurements they take, and whether to repeat these measurements. Where appropriate, encourage them to repeat their measurements to obtain more accurate results. Prompt the pupils to consider how valid their data is: does it measure what it is meant to measure? If the data was collected again would it yield the same results? By the end of Key Stage 2 most of your pupils should be able to choose the equipment to make these measurements accurately and to record data using tables, bar charts, pie charts or line graphs. Pupils often find it difficult to interpret different types of graphs, especially line graphs. A useful strategy to adopt is to use the interactive white board to draw different types of lines on graphs including curved lines, or where the line may change shape or direction and ask the children to consider the relationship between the variables. Encourage the children to read off intermediate values in their graphs and even extrapolate outside the range in their graphs to help them make predictions. In your plenary, ask the children to evaluate their own graphs or comment on each other's, thinking of ways in which they could be further improved.

Explaining results is a vital stage of any enquiry and should be given high priority. Pupils need to use and develop their knowledge and understanding to explain the data they have collected. It is vital that they link their findings to their original hypothesis and see whether they were right or wrong. They should use relevant scientific language and illustrations to discuss, communicate and justify their scientific ideas and where necessary talk about how scientific ideas have developed over time.

This is your opportunity as a teacher to reinforce and extend the learning, so use your questions effectively to achieve this. Try using reasoning questions such as *How do you think this has happened?* or *How could we find out whether all planets orbit the Sun anti-clockwise?* Provide the pupils with opportunities not only to gather but also to reflect and discuss their data and comment on each other's data. Prompt them to be critical about the data they have collected, considering the weaknesses as well as the strengths in the data and ask them whether they would collect the data differently another time. They should use their results to identify when further tests and observations might be needed. Provide them with examples where they can see conclusions not supported by evidence and ask them to state why. Give the pupils opportunities to draw conclusions and then justify their conclusions. They should be able to recognise which secondary sources would be most useful to research their ideas and begin to separate an opinion from a fact.

The importance of talk

Talk is important in science education because by engaging pupils in speaking and listening, it helps pupils organise their thoughts and reinforces learning in science. Talk requires children to explain their scientific ideas to each other and makes sense of their ideas. It helps to reinforce or challenge their thinking and is a useful rehearsal for writing about their experiences. Mercer et al. (2004) note how we use language in our learning to make sense of our experiences and to represent our ideas. Talk also helps pupils to realise that their work is valued. Alexander's (2004) research on dialogic teaching discusses the different types of talk that can be observed in a primary classroom and the need for children and teachers to listen carefully and respond to each other. This is often described as exploratory talk where all pupils give their ideas, treat each other's ideas with respect and share information. In science there are many opportunities for talk while pupils are asking questions, investigating a model or carrying out their scientific enquiries and reporting their results. Pupil–pupil interaction is thus important as well as teacher–pupil interaction. Your role is crucial in helping children develop their ideas based on concepts already formed and used to make sense of new ideas, and this can be achieved through talk and using questions. Talk and discussion provide the opportunity to challenge pupils' misconceptions too in order to move the learning forward. Talk will also provide you with useful assessment information to plan pupils' next steps in learning. The new national curriculum reiterates the importance of the spoken language and its significance in pupils' development from cognitive, social and linguistic points of view. It underlines how the quality and variety of language that pupils hear and speak are key factors in developing their scientific vocabulary and helping them articulate science concepts clearly.

While engaging in talk it is important to take children's ideas into account. The constructivist view of learning (Vygotsky, 1962), describes how learners construct their own meaning based on ideas or concepts already formed, to make sense of new ideas. These ideas can then be tested out. Even though children come to school from different cultural backgrounds and with different experiences, research such as the SPACE (Science, Processes and Concepts Exploration) project (1990–98) shows that there is much similarity in the ideas children have to explain the world around them. It is useful for you as the teacher to know what these ideas are and what misconceptions children might have on the topic you are teaching, which will guide you in the learning objectives that you set and the activities that you plan for the children. Your role is crucial in finding out what these ideas are and then helping children to develop these ideas by undertaking different enquiries and prompting them to reflect on their understanding. Each main chapter in this book highlights the common misconceptions that pupils might have in relation to a specific topic and acts as a useful starting point for you to work from. Children need to be active in their own learning and can scaffold each other's learning through discussion, when for example working in groups.

Scientific enquiry and the ability of children to work scientifically provide children with the opportunities to find answers to their questions, develop their knowledge of scientific concepts and make sense of their world. Your role as a teacher is essential in providing opportunities for enquiries to take place, scaffolding the learning and modelling the use of talk to enable this to happen. Science also promotes important skills and attitudes and thus has a fundamental role to play in the twenty-first century primary curriculum.

Critical questions

» *Reflect on your own teaching and try to explain how you synthesise the dual aspect of science.*

» *What strategies will you put in place to encourage a range of enquiries in your classroom?*

» *Identify the specific areas of scientific enquiry where you feel less confident and think about how you might build your competence.*

» *How will you promote the use of talk in science?*

Taking it further

Harlen, W (2005) *Teaching, Learning and Assessing Science 5–12*, 4th Edition. London: Paul Chapman Publishing.

Harlen, W (2006) *ASE Guide to Primary Science Education*. Hatfield: Association for Science Education.

Watson, JR, Goldsworthy, A and Wood-Robinson, V (1988) *ASE-King's Science Investigations in Schools (AKSIS) Project: Second Interim Report to the QCA*. London: Kings College.

References

Alexander, R (2004) *Towards Dialogic Teaching: Rethinking Classroom Talk*. York: Dialogos.

DfE (2013) *Teachers' Standards*. www.gov.uk/government/uploads/system/uploads/attachment_data/file/208682/Teachers__Standards_2013.pdf (accessed 17 February 2014).

Education Reform Act 1988. www.legislation.gov.uk/ukpga/1988/40/contents (accessed 18 February 2014).

Mercer, N, Dawes, L, Wegerif, R and Sams, C (2004) Reasoning as a Scientist: Ways of Helping Children to Use Language to Learn Science. *British Educational Research Journal*, 30(3), 359–77.

SPACE (Science Processes and Concepts Exploration) Research Reports (1990–98). Liverpool: Liverpool University Press.

Vygotsky, LS (1962) *Thought and Language*. Cambridge, MA: MIT Press.

2 What makes an effective science lesson?

Introduction

An effective science lesson is not only an excellent science lesson, but one that is superior to others and stands out from the rest. Difficult science concepts are taught in an inspiring and effective manner, pupils are actively involved in their learning and the environment is highly stimulating, leading to excellent levels of motivation, commitment and achievement by pupils. This chapter explores those elements that contribute to making a science lesson effective and in doing so will make reference to both the Teachers' Standards (DfE, 2013) and Ofsted Criteria (2014). It is very important that before you embark on your teaching of science, you ensure that you possess very good pedagogical and subject knowledge. This will enable you to explain scientific concepts to children and choose from a combination of teaching strategies to achieve your objectives. Communicating enthusiasm for science and relating your science to the children's experiences as much as possible is also essential for effective teaching and learning to take place. Enthusing your pupils so that they enjoy the subject, as well as having high expectations, is also vital.

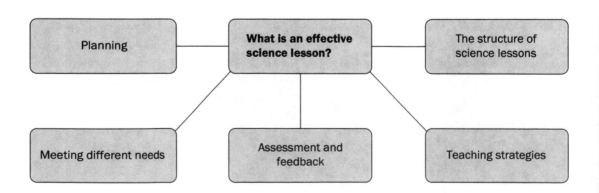

Teaching strategies

Teaching strategies are the different approaches that teachers use to improve their pupils' learning. These may consist of interactive, practical demonstrations or using secondary sources of information to achieve the learning objectives. There is no one correct strategy to use and it is best to adopt the notion of fitness for purpose. When evaluating the quality of teaching in a lesson, Ofsted (2014) will be looking to see whether the teaching strategies being used are well judged and appropriate to the needs of the children in that class. Standard 4 of the Teachers' Standards is concerned with the planning and teaching of well-structured lessons, how the teacher imparts knowledge and develops understanding through effective use of lesson time and promotes a love of learning and children's intellectual curiosity.

Ensure there is active learning in your science lesson where pupils are not passively listening. Thus plan your lesson to maximise pupil interaction and avoid too much talking from the front. This will improve children's understanding and retention of scientific knowledge and develop their problem-solving skills.

Ensure your science lessons provide opportunities for children to engage in practical/investigative work, where the children can work scientifically (National Curriculum, DfE, 2013), for example, finding out which is the strongest magnet or designing and making a switch to incorporate into a circuit. Promote inquiry-based learning where children arrive at an understanding of the concept by themselves.

Having the children work in groups can very often promote discussion which will enable them to deepen their learning and develop their own views as well as listening to those of others. Bennett (1995) suggested that the ideal size for groups who were involved in collaborative work was four and that mixed-gender and mixed-ability groups tended to generate a range of ideas and be more focused. Therefore, change the membership of the groups to allow children to work with those of different as well as similar abilities. Encourage independence, give time for thinking and discussion, and establish some ground rules so that children listen to each other's points of view, take turns and allow everyone the opportunity to speak.

Use imaginative and innovative resources to engage the children and avoid relying on a narrow range of resources. Using ICT can help children access, select and interpret information, or test the reliability and accuracy of data. Use secondary sources of information such as books to carry out some research on the work of Darwin with Year 6 pupils. The use of the outside environment can help children to appreciate the wide range of plants and animals found there. Outside visits, for example to a science museum, or inviting a visiting expert into the classroom can give children a different perspective of the topic. Models and analogies might be useful to explain difficult concepts (see Chapter 7 (Earth and space) or Chapter 12 (Electricity) for some ideas). Consider using games or simulations in your teaching. Using these will allow children to understand complex scientific ideas such as the apparent movement of the Sun across the sky, or the different food chains found in an ecosystem. At times you may need to carry out a demonstration yourself, especially if there are health and safety implications, for example showing condensation by placing a cold plate over a boiling kettle. Also, think carefully of how children will record their science work. This may include cartoons, poetry or drama. Decide whether it is essential that children write everything down or whether photographs can be used as alternatives and try not to over-use worksheets.

Make connections between the science topic under discussion and other topics in science; for example if teaching about floating and sinking link to the properties of materials. Try to link science to other areas of the curriculum too. If teaching about healthy eating, link to design and technology and the work being done on making a healthy sandwich. The new national curriculum (DfE, 2013) stresses the importance of children using technical terminology accurately and precisely and building up an extended specialist vocabulary. Thus remember to use subject-specific vocabulary effectively and display this in the classroom so children can learn and use it.

Critical questions

After teaching your science lesson, assess the teaching strategies that you used by asking yourself the following questions.

» *Was the lesson interactive and multi-sensory?*

» *Did you judge well when to intervene and when to allow the children to apply previously taught strategies?*

» *Was there evidence of learning and not just consolidation?*

» *Were there opportunities for children to engage in discussion to develop their ideas?*

Planning

An effective science lesson should be underpinned by careful planning to take account of children's prior experience and stage of development and build on their capabilities and prior knowledge (Teachers' Standards 2). Before you plan your science scheme for the next term, refer to your school's long-term plans to see where your science topic fits in with your current year group and class and note what has been covered previously. This will ensure progression in learning. Your science lessons should take account of children's common misconceptions in the topic being taught and you should try to teach in a way that will tackle these misconceptions and not aggravate them. You should give careful thought to how you will simplify scientific ideas while retaining the integrity of meaning. Ensure that you plan when and how you will introduce scientific terms in your lesson and make them accessible to children. Devise clear and manageable learning objectives based on the programmes of study of the national curriculum for science (DfE, 2013), and these should describe what the children are going to learn, not what they are going to do.

1. Two learning objectives, and a maximum of three, should suffice.

2. Display your learning objectives in your classroom and refer to them during the lesson.

3. Explain what your pupils are learning today (WALT) and what you are looking for (WILF).

Your learning objectives should also cover a combination of the following:

- basic skills to be learnt, such as using a Newton meter;

- procedural skills, such as controlling variables;

- concepts to be learnt, ie knowledge and understanding relating to the new national curriculum (DfE, 2013) programmes of study, for example *a completed circuit is required for a bulb to light*;

- use of correct and specific scientific terminology;

- positive attitudes, such as considering the ideas of others in the group.

Before the lesson, plan the questions you will ask the children in order to focus their attention on scientific ideas, processes and skills. Questions are essential for checking pupil understanding and making appropriate interventions.

Always consider any health and safety issues associated with the lesson. Identify potential hazards, assess risks and select safe ways to proceed. Refer to the ASE (2010) handbook, *Be Safe in Science*, and if in doubt always consult your science co-ordinator in school. At the end of each chapter in this book you will find a list of health and safety points to help you identify key areas for attention within that particular topic. It is a good idea to try out anything practical beforehand, eg ensuring that all your bulbs and batteries work to ensure the smooth running of your lesson.

Critical questions

After teaching your science lesson, review and reflect by asking yourself the following questions.

» *Did your teaching enable the pupils to make connections with previous learning and what was the impact of your teaching on the children's learning? (Teachers' Standards 2)*

» *Did you anticipate and overcome any barriers to learning or potential misconceptions during your lesson? (Teachers' Standards 3)*

» *Were you secure in your subject knowledge? (Teachers' Standards 3)*

The structure of science lessons

An effective science lesson will have a clear structure that includes an introduction, main activity and plenary.

Introduction

The introduction to your lesson is your opportunity to inform the children of what they will be learning and revise any science concepts covered in previous lessons. It may be an opportunity for you to explain new science concepts or introduce new scientific vocabulary. It is vital that children participate in this part of the lesson, for example by answering questions, talking to a partner or perhaps helping with a demonstration. Maintain the pace during this part of the lesson and briskly move to the next part of the lesson, making effective use of time (Teachers' Standards 4). Make sure you explain any key words in your learning objectives which pupils may be unsure of, such as friction or force. Thinking of a way to stimulate interest at the start of the lesson and command attention, for example showing pupils an interesting artefact or taking them on a short walk round the school to see which items use electricity, will result in pupils being engaged from the outset. When evaluating the quality of teaching, Ofsted (2014), for example, will look to see whether teachers and other adults are creating a positive climate for learning in which pupils are interested and engaged. Remember to elicit pupils' understanding to help them make connections between new and existing knowledge. This may be done through questioning the children.

Main activity

This part of the lesson allows you to continue working on ideas already introduced, but also provides the opportunity to introduce new ideas. Think of your role and how you will use your time effectively to maximise learning. This is your opportunity to instruct, demonstrate, explain and illustrate ideas and skills. If children are having difficulty, carry out a mini-plenary by stopping the class and reviewing what has been done up to now. Deal with any misconceptions or problems, show examples of good practice and focus them on the next steps in their learning. If children are working in groups ensure these are a manageable size (between four to six groups each with four to six pupils usually works well) and think about how you will share your time between the groups. You may decide to work with a focus group and oversee the rest of the pupils. You may decide to move between the different groups during the lesson, assessing understanding. If you have classroom support ensure that they have been briefed before the lesson and they are aware of the learning outcomes for the group they are working with. Move your classroom support around when teaching different science lessons so they do not always work with the same group. Ensure that you and any other adults in your class generate high levels of engagement with the children. Always think about the timings of the various parts of the lesson so pupils have sufficient time to complete their science activity.

Plenary

Provide time for discussion and reviewing work during this important part of the lesson, as this is your opportunity to summarise and review the learning. Recap what has been taught and what pupils should have learnt. Tackle any misconceptions and encourage children to reflect on their learning, perhaps by carrying out some form of self-assessment or engaging them in peer review. The latter is a skill that may need to be prompted or scaffolded with questions; for example list two things you like about how a group recorded their results and one thing that could be improved, such as the labelling of both axes in a graph.

Meeting different needs

It is important that you respond to the individual needs of your pupils while teaching science and know when and how to differentiate appropriately using approaches which enable pupils to be taught effectively. Standard 1 of the Teachers' Standards asks teachers to set goals that stretch and challenge pupils of all backgrounds, abilities and dispositions, and Standard 5 requires teachers to adapt teaching to respond to the strengths and needs of all pupils. When planning your science lesson, consider how you will support your less able pupils and extend your more able pupils and provide extra help for those with special requirements, such as those with English as an additional language (EAL). Effective matching of a task to an individual's need is complex and ongoing. Bearne (1996) states that differentiation is about having a flexible approach to learning, where a teacher is able to use a wide range of teaching strategies so that the learning is made accessible and embraces the diversity of all pupils. No single approach is used all the time and you will need to choose which approach best fits the task and the needs of your learners at that particular time.

There are a variety of means of maximising learning for all children and taking account of the diversity of pupils' knowledge, their experiences and how they approach learning. These include:

- differentiating by task;
- differentiating by support;
- differentiating by resources;
- differentiating by outcome.

Differentiating by task

You may decide to differentiate by task and give children different activities in your science lesson; for example the less able pupils might be asked to build a circuit using a bulb, a cell and some wires. Your average ability might be investigating which materials are conductors and let electricity flow through and which are insulators and do not allow electricity to flow through. Your more able pupils might be designing and making a switch to incorporate into their circuit. This type of approach may be very effective in matching the task to the diverse needs of the children but will require a wide range of resources and may result in labelling children as they are organised into ability groups.

Differentiating by support

This entails pupils of different abilities being helped in accessing, interpreting or completing their task by, for example, modifying the support offered by the adults, the materials and the pupils' peers. Children could work in mixed-ability groupings on an investigation to find out which surface has the greatest friction, with the more able pupils supporting the less able and scaffolding each other's learning. Provide opportunities for children to engage in discussion to develop their ideas. You could have your Teaching Assistant working with the more able pupils to extend their learning further, for example when understanding a difficult topic such as the phases of the Moon. Ensure your Teaching Assistant is used with all ability groups in your class and that your more able pupils are also being challenged in order to maximise their learning.

Differentiating by resources

Another way in which you may differentiate your science lesson is by the use of resources. Your more able group might measure force using a Newton meter, while your less able group might be given a writing frame to help them record their investigations. Again, this type of support will require a range of materials and resources and will restrict the resources that are provided for certain pupils.

Consider how you can differentiate your open and closed questioning during the introduction or plenary of the lesson to develop higher order thinking skills and to cater for the needs of different children in your class.

Differentiating by outcome

In some instances you may decide that your science task is open ended, such as a problem-solving activity or an investigation, eg which material will be the most hard wearing, and you will expect a different outcome from your different groups where performance will be judged using specific criteria, eg the accuracy or use of technical vocabulary. Differentiation by outcome is thus based on the variable amount and quality of work produced by different pupils who have been set precisely the same task.

Critical questions

After teaching your science lesson, consider the following.

» *How did you differentiate and meet the needs of all ability levels?*

» *Was your method successful and how do you judge and measure this success?*

» *Were all pupils engaged during the science activity?*

» *Did you judge well when to intervene to move the children on with their learning and when to allow the children to apply previously taught strategies?*

Assessment and feedback

Planning for assessment and giving pupils appropriate and useful feedback which will enhance learning is an essential ingredient of an effective science lesson. Standard 1 of the Teachers' Standards asks teachers to guide pupils to reflect on their progress and their emerging needs, and Standard 6 requires teachers to be able to make accurate and productive use of assessment. Assessment should be taking place at all points during your science lesson and you need to decide what you will assess, who you will assess and how. Identify clear success criteria to assess against, based on your learning objectives, and monitor children's progress during the lesson. You can assess understanding through questioning, listening and observing the pupils. Encourage the children to assess their own knowledge and understanding, to learn from their mistakes, and use your plenary effectively to reinforce your learning intentions at the outset. Provide children with feedback on their performance at all times during the lesson and make this feedback as formative as possible so pupils are clear about what they need to do next.

Assessment thus needs to be embedded into your practice, so that you and your pupils are consistently reviewing and reflecting on assessment information to inform and change future teaching and learning. These assessments will be essential in informing your next science lesson.

Critical questions

An effective teacher should always reflect on their practice, so consider the following points after each of your science lessons.

» *Did you monitor and record the impact of your teaching on pupils' progress over time and have you adjusted your teaching at individual, group and class levels accordingly as a result?*

» *Did you give children appropriate feedback in respect of their learning?*

» *Do you know what to plan next for the children?*

Taking it further

Griffith, A and Burns, M (2012) *Outstanding Teaching: Engaging Learners*. Carmarthen: Crown House Publishing.

Ofsted (2013) *Maintaining Curiosity: A Survey into Science Education in Schools*. Manchester: Crown Publications.

Robinson, C, Bingle, B and Howard, C (2013) *Primary School Placements: A Critical Guide to Outstanding Teaching*. Northwich: Critical Publishing.

References

ASE (2010) *Be Safe in Science*, 4th Edition. Hatfield: ASE.

Bearne, E (ed.) (1996) *Differentiation and Diversity in the Primary School*. London: Routledge.

Bennett, N (1995) Managing Learning through Group Work, in C Deforges (ed.) *An Introduction to Teaching: Psychological Perspectives*. Oxford: Blackwell.

DfE (2013) *Teachers' Standards*. www.gov.uk/government/uploads/system/uploads/attachment_ data/file/208682/Teachers__Standards_2013.pdf (accessed 17 February 2014).

Ofsted (2014) *The Framework for School Inspection*. Manchester: Crown Publications.

3 Animals and humans

Introduction

As children start to grow they will become aware firstly of the animals that surround them and then of the variety of livings things that can be found on our planet. Pupils will start to identify similarities and differences among species and will discover and learn that all living things, like humans, have a variety of needs in order for them to breed, flourish and survive.

Children should also develop a growing awareness of themselves as human beings, be able to name the basic parts of the human body and recognise that they have senses to help them understand the world around them. As they grow older they will start to appreciate the functions the parts of our body play in supporting and sustaining life and how our lifestyle choices can ultimately affect our health and even our ability to survive.

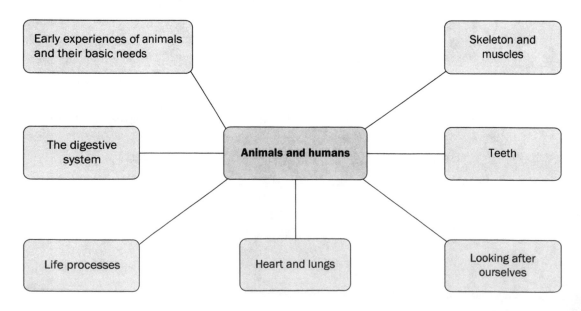

KEY VOCABULARY

The new national curriculum (DfE, 2013) stresses the importance of children using technical terminology accurately and precisely and building up an extended specialist vocabulary.

In Key Stage 1 children will have started to use vocabulary to label the basic parts of the human body, such as the **head**, **neck**, **arms**, **elbows**, **legs**, **knees**, **face**, **hair**, **mouth** and **teeth**. They will also realise that our **eyes, ears, hands, nose** and **tongue** provide us with information using our **senses**. Pupils will recognise that animals and humans have **offspring** that grow into adults and that all living things have similar basic needs to flourish including **food, water** and, for some living things, **air**. Children should also become aware that by eating the right foods and by exercising they can stay healthy and grow. Children will have been taught about the need for **hygiene** from an early age and this will now start to become an increasingly important part of growing older.

During Key Stage 2, you should continue to develop pupils' vocabulary linked to the topic of animals and humans.

Children will be taught to think about the important role that **nutrition** plays in their daily lives and how the diets of humans and animals have similarities and differences. They will learn about the purpose of the basic human **digestive system** and encounter vocabulary such as **oesophagus, stomach** and **small and large intestines**. Children should be taught the role that teeth, including **incisors, canines** and **molars**, play in making food edible. Pupils will be made aware of the functions of a **skeleton** and **muscles**, and other **organs** such as the **heart, lungs, kidneys, liver, arteries** and **veins**. Children should also be taught that while some animals have skeletons, other creatures can exist without one or with an **exoskeleton**.

With a developed awareness of basic anatomy pupils should learn about the **circulatory system** in order to describe the function of the **heart, blood vessels** and **blood**. This will help them understand how nutrients and water are transported around the body of living things. They will learn that the body changes as they get older and this is linked to **puberty** and how we, like some other animals, have a **gestation period**. They will also need to be made aware of the harm that lifestyle choices can have on their bodies and of the effects of **drugs** and **exercise**.

CHILDREN'S IDEAS AND COMMON MISCONCEPTIONS

Children may hold various misconceptions about animals and humans:

*   animals may only be seen as pets;
*   animals inside eggs are completely formed;
*   animals is a term used for all living creatures;
*   washing ourselves is only beneficial in terms of keeping us clean.

As children progress through Key Stage 2 the following misconceptions may still occur:

- all animals need a skeleton;
- all animals have the same teeth as humans;
- about the size and location of the heart, lungs, liver and kidneys;
- why we have blood and how it moves around the body;
- food does not consist of other food groups;
- our blood is blue;
- air breathed in or out is just part of living and has no purpose;
- the air we breathe out is mainly carbon dioxide with little oxygen;
- our stomach is something very compact and is to be found low down in our body;
- animals carry their young for the same time as humans.

Topics and teaching strategies

Early experiences of animals

In Year 1 children are expected to

> *describe and compare the structure of a variety of common animals (fish, amphibians, reptiles, birds and mammals, including pets.*
>
> (DfE, 2013, page 149)

By taking pupils outside to explore their local environments they can experience a variety of living things from creatures that inhabit the soil, such as worms and centipedes, to the animals that live in and around their school's nature area and pond, such as frogs, newts and tadpoles. Start to ask children why these creatures live in such habitats and help them understand how to respect living things that they may have collected to observe so that they will return these creatures safely after study.

By inviting parents or other adults to bring small, safe animals, such as puppies and rabbits, into the classroom young children can start to learn about how to look after pets by feeding them and caring for their needs. Your school may also allow class pets. Ask pupils to bring in photos of their own pets so that they can also share how they care for their own animals. You can also approach your local vet or veterinary nurse to see if they will come to talk to the pupils about more unusual pets, or ask them if you can arrange a visit to their surgery to see how they care for animals.

While studying all these animals encourage pupils to name their characteristic features; so, for example, a chicken has wings, feathers, a beak and eyes and lays eggs. This will help children to realise that groups of creatures have similar features and that some have features like our own, such as a neck, ears and mouth. Demonstrate how different parts of the body have particular functions by asking children to take part in *Follow My Leader* games or you can use action songs such as *Heads, Shoulders, Knees and Toes* to help them identify their own body parts.

Children in Year 1 should also be able to

identify, name, draw and label the basic parts of the human body and say which part of the body is associated with each sense.

(DfE, 2013, page 149)

By discussing, for example, the sense of smell with children they will be able to see how the nose helps us find out about our environment and what is pleasurable or not. Ask children to see if they can identify smells, such as flowers and chocolate, when blindfolded. Draw parallels with a dog which uses its nose and sense of smell to find objects and locate food.

Help children to name the more familiar creatures they may encounter, such as worms, caterpillars and cats. See if they can tell you about the features of these creatures and how they might live. By collecting and giving pupils a range of photographs you can see if they can start sorting and grouping (*working scientifically*) these living creatures by characteristics such as how many legs they have and where they live.

Basic needs

As children move into Year 2 the new national curriculum suggests that pupils should progress to

notice that animals, including humans, have offspring which grow into adults.

(DfE, 2013, page 152)

Pupils will have started to become aware of how humans and animals change from birth into adulthood. They are often fascinated by baby animals such as chicks. You could promote this interest by asking them to sort pictures of animals and humans at differing ages or asking pupils to bring in photographs of themselves or their pets during different stages of their lives. Get children to focus on features that help them recognise growth, such as the animals' sizes or the growth of flight feathers. By observing animals brought into school you can get pupils to make direct comparisons with how they have changed with age. You can also get children to draw and measure both humans and animals as they grow in order to create first-hand observations (*working scientifically*).

Encourage pupils to learn the names of the developmental stages of living things, for example egg, chick and chicken, or baby, toddler, child, teenager and adult. You can extend their study to more complex life cycles such as egg, caterpillar, pupa and butterfly.

Children in Year 2 should also:

- *find out about and describe the basic needs of animals, including humans, for survival (water, food and air);*

   -    *describe the importance for humans of exercise, eating the right amounts of different types of food, and hygiene.*

                                          (DfE, 2013, page 152)

By observing and caring for animals in school and at home pupils will realise that these creatures need food and water in order that they survive.

Pupils themselves also need to drink plenty of fluid either from their own lunch flask or through water bottles provided at school. You should explain to pupils that water is present in all our cells and that it is needed to aid our circulation, digestion and to remove waste and toxins from our bodies. Since water is lost when people sweat or perspire it is important that your pupils understand the need to replace it.

Encourage pupils to look at the range of food that animals need to survive. By getting children to safely fill bird feeders, to feed the fish in the pond or even to feed themselves they will get first-hand experience of the range of foods different species eat. Looking at the range of foods in lunchboxes can be useful. By discussing how too much of one thing is not good for children you can start to make them aware of the need for a balanced diet.

You should enforce basic hygiene rules, like washing hands, when handling or eating foods. This can extend into other aspects of their school lives, such as wiping their noses or not sharing drinking cups, and will help children realise that good hygiene is necessary to keep them healthy and reduce the spread of diseases.

Draw attention to pupils' feelings when they are exercising or playing outside. Ask them *Do you feel your heart beating now?* and highlight the links between exercise and health.

The study of nutrition should be extended as children get older, so they can

> *identify that animals, including humans, need the right types and amount of nutrition, and that they cannot make their own food; they get nutrition from what they eat.*

                                          (DfE, 2013, page 158)

You should also make clear the needs of animals to eat the right amounts and types of food by introducing the food groups.

FACTFILE

The best sources of protein are found in meat, fish, eggs, dairy products, nuts, seeds, beans and lentils. Proteins help build, replace and maintain healthy body tissues such as muscles.

Vitamins and minerals are found in all foods and are needed to help the body work properly and to grow. Each vitamin plays an important role in the body: for example Vitamin D in milk helps bones develop and Vitamin C in oranges helps the body repair itself if it gets injured.

Carbohydrates are broken down by the body to produce sugars which provide a major source of energy for the body. Simple carbohydrates can be obtained from refined sugars and fruit, while complex carbohydrates (starches) are found in foods such as bread, pasta and rice.

By getting children to read the food labels on packets they will come across a variety of terms linked to nutrition. Encourage them to research using secondary sources what these terms mean and why the body needs them. Ensure your pupils are introduced to all the main food types. Get them to look at the diet of athletes to see how their dietary requirements are different and provide the energy they need to perform well in their chosen sport. You could even ask children to name their favourite food and ask them to predict how eating too much of this one food may affect them both in the short and long term.

Skeleton and muscles

As children get older there is a need to extend their knowledge to learning about the anatomy of living creatures. As the new curriculum suggests, pupils should

> *identify that humans and some other animals have skeletons and muscles for support, protection and movement.*
>
> (DfE, 2013, page 158)

If you have one available show the children a model skeleton, or use a poster, and ask them if they can identify any major bones. Many children will be familiar with terms such as ribs and skull and know where they are in the body, but help them to name less familiar bones. Get them to think about why we have a rib cage, why we have bones in our legs and why we have a backbone. Encourage them to find the bones you are discussing in their bodies. See if any children have had broken limbs and ask them to tell others what happens when a bone is fractured.

Contrast our skeletons with those of other animals. Ask pupils to describe any similarities and differences that they can see. Get children to think about animals such as jellyfish which have no skeletons. How do they get around and what happens to their appearance when they get washed up on shore, given their lack of skeleton? Ask the children if there is anything to stop the organs inside the jellyfish from being crushed if they were trodden on. These discussions will draw out how skeletons support the body, assist movement and protect our organs. You can extend children's understanding of skeletons by showing them pictures of a crab, where the exoskeleton serves a similar purpose to that of our human skeleton.

Children can make simple hinge and ball and socket joints, as shown in Figure 3.1, so that they can see for themselves the role our bones and joints have in helping us move. This study will also help children realise that attached to our bones are muscles which play a very important part in helping us move.

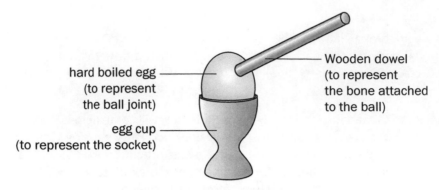

Model of a ball and socket joint

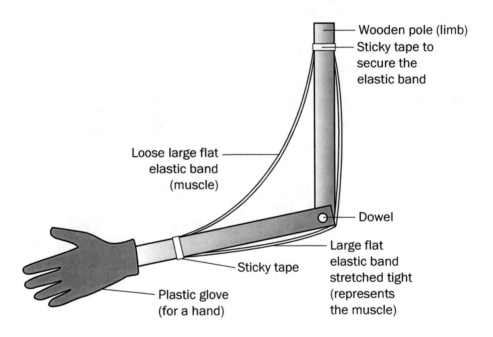

Model of a hinge joint

Figure 3.1 *Models of a ball and socket joint and a hinge joint*

FACTFILE

Muscles form three groups.

1. Skeletal muscles are attached to the bones of the skeleton and are voluntary muscles because we can make them work by our conscious thinking. Examples of these muscles include the biceps and triceps which help raise and lower our arms. Muscles such as the arm muscles are also called antagonistic pairs of muscles, since as one contracts the other relaxes.

2.   Smooth muscles are involuntary muscles and may be found in the stomach wall to help us digest food and in the iris of the eye to help us open and close our pupils.

3.   Cardiac muscles are involuntary muscles located around the heart. It is these muscles which allow for the regular contractions of the heart.

Ask children to look at their faces in mirrors and see if they can identify where the muscles might be to make parts of their face move. Ask them to feel the muscles on their body such as their calf muscles or biceps. Get them to think about moving their arms and how their muscles feel during this movement. By attaching elastic bands to the simple hinge joint in Figure 3.1 they will be able to see how muscles help move our limbs and also help them return to their normal position, due to their antagonistic nature. Encourage children to realise that skeletal muscles are moved voluntarily, by us thinking about movement.

Now get pupils to consider if we have muscles that we cannot see. Does the heart have muscles? Do we actively think to make these muscles move or do they move without us thinking about it? If so, why is this the case? This can lead you on to a discussion about the importance of the cardiac muscles. Ask children if they can think of any other involuntary muscles, for example, how does the food move through our stomach and what sort of muscles are these?

The digestive system

Children in Year 4 need to learn about the major organs within the human body, including the stomach:

> describe the simple functions of the basic parts of the digestive system in humans.

> (DfE, 2013, page 162)

To start this topic you should encourage children to look at an anatomical torso which your school will almost certainly have or alternatively you could borrow from your feeder high school. They could also look at photographs of the stomach to help children start to learn what organs are inside their human body.

FACTFILE

The stomach provides a means to digest foods and liquids which have been eaten. Once a meal is placed into the mouth it is cut up and chewed by the teeth into smaller pieces if necessary. Once swallowed the food and liquids, together with the saliva, go down into the oesophagus which transports the food into the stomach. The stomach uses enzymes and acid to start breaking down the proteins in the food. After being in the stomach the food moves on to the small intestine and then the large intestine which digests and absorbs the food into the body.

You can get children to locate their stomach by firstly helping them find the base of their breastbones. Then get them to place their flat palm with the thumb upward touching the breastbone's base. This will indicate approximately where their stomach is located and how big it is. Explain to them that the stomach is just one part of the digestive system. You will need to help them understand that it is preceded by the oesophagus and that the small and large intestines are tubes that follow on from the stomach. The purpose of this digestive system is to break down and process our food so that we can fuel our bodies.

Teeth

Children need to understand how important our teeth are in the processing of our food. Children in Year 4 are therefore required in the new curriculum to

> *identify the different types of teeth in humans and their simple functions.*
>
> (DfE, 2013, page 162)

Young children will be aware of their teeth from an early age as their milk teeth fall out and are replaced as they grow older, and because they should all regularly visit a dentist.

FACTFILE

Before children get to their first birthday they start to get their first teeth, called milk teeth. A child will have approximately 20 baby teeth well before they start school. By the time children have moved into the lower juniors these teeth will have started to fall out and will be replaced by permanent teeth. Humans have 32 permanent teeth which include canines for ripping and tearing food, incisors for biting off and chewing and molars for crushing and grinding food. Wisdom teeth are the large molars found at the back, on the top and bottom, of each jaw.

Children will have looked in their mouth to locate their 'wobbly tooth' and grown familiar with how their teeth are changing with age. To develop children's understanding of this topic use mirrors to look inside their mouths and to help identify and then draw the variety of teeth they can see. Ask them if any of their pets have similar-looking teeth. Using images or secondary sources you can also get children to research what teeth other animals have and why. Through discussion you will be able to help them understand the purpose of canines, incisors and molars. Ask children about their own experiences of going to the dentist and about having fillings or possibly even extractions. This will quickly lead you on to the topic of the need to brush teeth to remove bacteria and sugar found in plaque that forms around their teeth. You can use model teeth to show children how to correctly brush their teeth or organise for the local dental hygienist or school nurse to come into school to discuss oral hygiene. To impress on children the need to protect their teeth from sugary or acidic snacks, place a boiled egg into orange juice or a cola drink and leave for a few days.

Life processes

In Year 3, the new curriculum expects children to:

- *describe the life processes of reproduction in some plants and animals;*

- *describe the changes as humans develop to old age.*

(DfE, 2013, page 168)

Children in their formative years will have studied how animals and humans change over time. You could now ask children to create a visual timeline for both animals and humans from birth to old age using images brought into school of their family or of their pets or by sourcing images through secondary research. Encourage the children to name the young of animals and to see that reproduction is needed so that a species can continue to exist and thrive in the future. By using first-hand experiences gained from visits to places, such as a farm or farm park or to a butterfly house, children can see how animals have young which in turn will grow up and have further offspring. To help children discover how humans develop over time encourage them to research into how humans develop in their mother's womb. They can then use secondary sources to compare gestation periods of humans and animals.

This topic can be revisited and developed as children progress into the upper juniors. By using secondary sources both in science and when studying 'relationships and sex education', which is often embedded in personal, social, health and economic education (PSHE), you will be able to discuss with children how our bodies alter and change as we get older, ready for adulthood and in preparation for sexual reproduction. This study will also allow pupils to develop a deepening knowledge of puberty.

The human heart and lungs

In Year 6, the new curriculum expects children to:

- *identify and name the main parts of the human circulatory system, and describe the functions of the heart, blood vessels and blood;*

- *describe the ways in which nutrients and water are transported within animals, including humans.*

(DfE, 2013, page 172)

FACTFILE

The heart is a very strong muscle that pumps blood around the body. It consists of four chambers, two upper chambers and two lower chambers, which squeeze the blood into and out of your heart and then around your body. The tubes that transport blood away from your heart are called arteries and the tubes that carry blood back towards your heart are called veins. Your pulse indicates how fast your heart is beating. Your heart will beat faster or slower depending on how rested you are.

The lungs are part of the breathing system and allow for air to move in and out of the body. The heart pumps blood to the lungs where it picks up oxygen from the air we have inhaled.

The kidneys are located at the bottom of the ribcage at the back of the body. These fist-sized, dark red organs are responsible for making urine from the waste and surplus water in the blood.

The liver is found near the stomach to the right-hand side of the body. This dark red organ is wedge shaped and is used by the body to get rid of toxins such as drugs and alcohol and to control the blood's sugar levels. It also produces bile which helps break down the fats that have been eaten.

The heart

The study of the heart builds on pupils' previous learning about the skeleton, our muscles and digestive system. You could encourage children to draw the size and position of a heart on an image of a torso. Then see if the children can find their own hearts. Emphasise that the heart is not in the centre of the body but on the left-hand side.

Since children will have seen blood on cuts and grazes get them to think about its colour and that while our veins appear blue, blood is in fact red. Get them to look closely at their veins in their wrist and lower arms that are near to the surface of the skin. Explain that veins are there to carry used blood back to the heart while arteries are found deeper in our bodies and carry blood away from the heart. Using visual resources explain that there are special valves inside our hearts to manage this flow of blood and to stop it going the wrong way around our circulatory system.

Ask children to find their pulse either by putting their index finger on the inside of their wrist or by feeling on their neck just under their jawbone close to their ears. They could count the beats and calculate how many beats are made each minute. Explain that this is a resting rate since they are not exercising. Children can be encouraged to think about what doctors use to listen to our hearts or to a baby's heartbeat while in the mother's womb.

When you get children to exercise they will quickly feel their hearts beat faster. Ask them to record their pulse rates and then to take several readings at 5 minute intervals. Ask them to predict what will happen to their heart rate and why, and to display their records using a line graph (*working scientifically*) or by using a spreadsheet. Encourage them to discuss how their muscles are now working harder so the heart beats faster to allow the blood to flow faster around the body, providing a greater supply of oxygen to keep them moving. It also means that the blood can deliver food to our bodies more quickly.

Ask children to consider whether all animals have hearts to help them move blood, oxygen and nutrients around their bodies.

The new national curriculum (DfE, 2013) does not directly mention the kidneys and liver as part of this topic; however it is important that they are discussed so that pupils understand their role in our life processes. You can get children to use secondary sources to research these organs or even ask them to draw and label them on a picture of a torso along with the other major organs in living things.

The lungs

Though not part of the new curriculum (DfE, 2013) this topic is important so that children understand how human lungs provide our bodies with oxygen, how this is circulated by our hearts and is needed to help us survive. Children with asthma will be all too aware of how shortness of breath impacts upon their ability to do exercise. See if they will talk about how their illness affects their lives.

By using video clips, such as those from BBC Learning Zone, about the heart and its function you aid children to understand the complex relationship that exists between the heart and the lungs and how it helps us to function as humans.

Looking after ourselves

Pupils in Year 6 should

> recognise the impact of diet, exercise, drugs and lifestyle on the way their bodies function.

(DfE, 2013, page 172)

Children will be aware of a range of medicines and drugs that can help them when they are ill but they must also learn about the relationship between their diet and how much they exercise, and how the taking of drugs such as alcohol and nicotine will impact upon their health.

Ask children to complete a questionnaire about their eating and exercise habits. Then ask them to compare what they have written with others who they feel comfortable talking to. See if they feel they are eating too many fatty foods or if they are doing enough exercise. Ask them to consider what effect a poor diet or lack of exercise could have on their lives. Using food packaging or the internet they could also be asked to research the amount of sugar or calories they have eaten in a day and what happens if they consume too many. Similarly, using secondary sources pupils could research about ways of keeping fit and its benefits. They can even be asked to find out if too much exercise is bad for them.

Nicotine and alcohol

Most children will be aware of smoking and drinking alcohol and will have seen them used by adults in their lives. Encourage children to research the drugs associated with these items and to discuss what they already know about them. Help them to see how harmful they can be to humans and the damage they can cause to our vital organs. You might like to discuss social attitudes to drinking and smoking and, through PSHE education, initiate a conversation about how pupils might be affected by them as they get older. You can also help them to consider strategies they might use to avoid taking them as a result of the peer pressures that they will inevitably face when they get older.

CROSS-CURRICULAR LINKS

There are many opportunities to promote cross-curricular links with this topic.

Literacy

Through extended pieces of persuasive writing or poster creation children can help others understand the need to live and eat healthily. Poems, shape poems, rhymes and alliteration about animals could be written by children to convey information about creatures and their movements. Pupils can be encouraged to create factfiles about skeletons, teeth and the organs of living things. Children could also be encouraged to keep a food, fitness and feelings diary to monitor how they are getting on in their daily lives. Instructional writing about how to brush teeth can also be promoted.

Numeracy

Numeracy can be promoted by looking at the use of measurements. Pupils can use metre and centimetre rulers and tape measures to record the size of their bodies and limbs. By using stop watches to record their pulse rates they can create detailed line graphs to show how their heart rate changes when exercising. They can also calculate daily calorie intakes.

Other curricular links

Art and design technology provides a visual means of exploring this topic. Three-dimensional models of teeth may be created alongside papier maché models of the torso and organs. You can also get children to design and create their own healthy sandwich.

History could cover how our approaches to medicine have changed over time and how scientists such as Pasteur helped identify and treat illnesses. Through a geographical study of developing countries children can learn how we need to make certain that clean water, food and medicines need to be available so that humans can lead healthy and prosperous lives.

In music, songs and rhymes, such as *Incy Wincy Spider*, *Baa Baa Black Sheep*, *Never Smile at a Crocodile* and *Five Little Ducks*, can be used to reinforce some characteristics of animals. Songs such as *Dem Bones* may also be used to help children remember and enjoy singing about the function of the human skeleton.

Through drama or in PE encourage children to mimic the movements of animals, such as slithering like snakes. In drama children can also be encouraged to have empathy with other age groups and to consider how our lives alter and change as we age.

HEALTH AND SAFETY

Remind children about the following key safety points:

- always wash hands properly when handling plants, animals, pond water and soil;

- germs are easily spread and open cuts or grazes should be covered. Disinfect shared objects such as straws;

- measure body temperature sensibly and always disinfect thermometers;

- some animals and plants can bite or sting;

- provide clear instructions for collecting and transporting animals, birds, bird nests and insects from the wild into the class and explain how to treat them and where to place them once they have been examined. Children should not bring dead animals into class;

- teeth should be sterilised before children handle them;

- avoid causing emotional or physical stress to participants during investigations into weight and appearance;

- children should avoid hazards found in the outside environment, such as broken glass, and stay within sight of the teacher at all times;

- raw meat, fish, eggs and nuts should not be brought into school;

- ensure food is stored and cooked appropriately;

- dispose of waste safely and appropriately;

- be aware of and sensitive to medical conditions or religious needs when handling foods or animals;

- when studying micro-organisms be aware of the harm and danger they can pose to health.

Critical questions

» On a scale of 1–10 (with 10 being completely confident) how confident do you now feel in your own subject knowledge about humans and animals?

» Identify the specific areas of the topic where you feel less confident.

» Where else might you look and what else might you do to develop your subject knowledge in those areas?

» What resources do you need to collect in order to successfully start teaching this topic?

Taking it further

Books

Chandler, F, Hancock, D and Woodcock, J (2004) *First Encyclopedia of the Human Body*. St Louis, MO: Turtleback Books.

Dorling Kindersley (2009) *The Concise Human Body Book: An Illustrated Guide to Its Structure, Function and Disorders*. London: Dorling Kindersley.

Winston, R (2005) *Body: An Amazing Tour of Human Anatomy*. London: Dorling Kindersley.

Websites

www.bbc.co.uk/bitesize/ks2/science/living_things/teeth_eating/read/1/ (accessed 5 February 2014).

www.bbc.co.uk/science/humanbody (accessed 5 February 2014).

www.nhs.uk/Livewell/dentalhealth/Pages/Careofkidsteeth.aspx (accessed 5 February 2014).

References

ASE (2010) *Be Safe in Science*, 4th Edition. Hatfield: ASE.

Daynes, K and King, K (Illustrator) (2006) *See Inside Your Body*. London: Osborne Publishing.

DfE (2013) *Teachers' Standards*. www.gov.uk/government/uploads/system/uploads/attachment_data/file/208682/Teachers__Standards_2013.pdf (accessed 17 February 2014).

4 Plants, habitats and living things

Introduction

Plants, habitats and living things is an area of science which can provide children with real experiences and use of the outdoor environment. This in turn will help them to understand life processes. Traditionally, the topics of plants and animals are treated separately, but they are dealt with together in this chapter to highlight the characteristics and interdependence of living things. Young children will be familiar with exploring and observing their local environment, using as much first-hand experience as possible and making use of all their senses in order to understand the world around them. As children get older they should progress to considering global habitats, the need to protect the environment and the importance of behaving in a sustainable way. This area of science can be linked to other subjects of the national curriculum, in particular geography, where issues such as recycling can be explored.

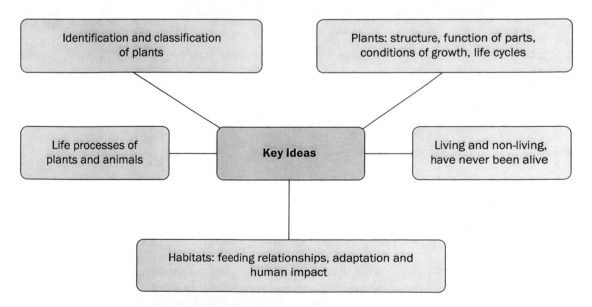

Identification and classification of plants

Plants: structure, function of parts, conditions of growth, life cycles

Life processes of plants and animals

Key ideas

Living and non-living, have never been alive

Habitats: feeding relationships, adaptation and human impact

KEY VOCABULARY

The new national curriculum (DfE, 2013) stresses the importance of children using technical terminology accurately and precisely and building up an extended specialist vocabulary.

In Key Stage 1 children should begin to learn basic vocabulary to describe plants and animals in their local environment. As they identify and name a variety of common plants and their basic structure, they need to learn about habitats and how plants and animals obtain their food, and the conditions for the growth of plants. During Years 1 and 2 children will become familiar with vocabulary such as **living, non-living, plant, trunk, branch, leaf, flower, blossom, petal, stem, root, shoot, fruit, bulb, seed, deciduous, evergreen, habitat, micro-habitat** and **food chain**. In Years 3 and 4 children will become familiar with vocabulary linked to the functions of different parts of flowering plants, conditions of growth, life cycles and changes to the local environment. This will entail pupils learning vocabulary such as **germination, nutrition, nutrient, reproduction, life cycle, pollination, seed formation, seed dispersal, vertebrate, invertebrate, fish, amphibian, reptile, bird** and **mammal**. It is in upper Key Stage 2, Years 5 and 6, that you will be required to continue to develop pupils' vocabulary linked to all living things and use key words such as **sexual** and **asexual reproduction, fertilisation, stigma, style, anther, filament, sepal, ovary, ovules, receptacle** and **micro-organisms**.

CHILDREN'S IDEAS AND COMMON MISCONCEPTIONS

During the study of this topic children will hold various misconceptions about plants, animals and living things. At an early age these may consist of the following:

- misunderstanding what is living and non-living and has never been alive, eg thinking a fire is living because it moves;

- all plants grow in a pot and have flowers with coloured petals, green leaves and a stem;

- a flower is the whole plant including petals, stem and leaves;

- plants only grow at night;

- all plants die during the winter;

- plants only get their food from the soil through their roots;

- soil is seen as a support rather than a source of water and nutrients;

- the function of the stem is to carry the food to the flower;

- children will mention water, sun and soil as conditions of growth for plants but rarely all three together;

- growth is seen as the unfolding of material in a seed rather than understanding that plants generate new materials from water and carbon dioxide;

- an animal is only a four-legged creature with fur;

- carnivorous equals savage.

Further misconceptions that may become apparent as children learn more about the topic are:

- the conditions for germination of seeds are the same as those for growth of plants;

- children think that plants get their food from the soil, eg nutrients, and find it difficult to understand that plants make their food using energy from the Sun;

- they think that the arrow in a food chain shows the direction of a predator rather than the flow of energy;

- misunderstanding the sequence of feeding and thinking that an animal feeds on all organisms below it in a food chain;

- children find it difficult to believe that all animals including humans ultimately depend on green plants for survival.

Topics and teaching strategies

Identification and classification of plants

The new curriculum suggests children need to:

- *identify and name a variety of common wild and garden plants, including deciduous and evergreen trees;*

- *identify and describe the basic structure of a variety of common flowering plants including trees.*

(DfE, 2013, page 148)

FACTFILE

A plant is a member of the kingdom Plantae comprising multi-cellular organisms that typically produce their own food by the process of photosynthesis and have more or less rigid cell walls.

A flower, sometimes known as a bloom or blossom, is the reproductive structure found in a flowering plant.

An ideal way for you to start this topic is to go for a walk with the children and get them observing the plants and trees that grow in their local environment. They could then be encouraged to extend their knowledge to include the common names of plants and flowers and be able to give examples of deciduous and evergreen trees, perhaps by also using secondary sources of information such as books. An interesting elicitation exercise which will help to find out children's ideas and focus your teaching is to use a collection of pictures of plants including weeds, plants not in flower, a tree and a cactus and ask them the question *What is a plant?*. This will hopefully help reinforce the teaching point that not all plants grow in a pot or have coloured petals or green leaves. They could also be asked to draw or write a list of as many plants as they can think of, including deciduous and evergreen. Older or more able children's thinking could be extended by asking them to draw flowering and non-flowering plants, plants found at home or plants whose parts are used as fruits or vegetables. Many children will have misconceptions about what is a plant or a flower so be ready to deal with these as is suggested later in the chapter.

You might extend children's knowledge of plants by asking the children to sort plants into different groups, thus developing their observation skills (*working scientifically*) or getting them to examine the size and shape of leaves that fall from the trees in the autumn. Magnifying glasses or digital microscopes can also be used. Children could then draw diagrams showing the different parts of the plants and trees to encourage them to record, or perhaps use digital photographs instead. They should be encouraged to observe the changes that occur over time and what happens during the different seasons, compare different plants and talk about how different plants change over time. Children need to appreciate that plants do live through winter too. Children will love to grow their own plants, flowers and vegetables and observe them as they grow. This is an ideal opportunity to reinforce key scientific vocabulary such as **flower**, **petal**, **stem**, **leaf**, **root**, **fruit**, **bulb** and **seed**. An exciting project might be to help with developing a school wildlife area. Local garden centres are often willing to help, supplying schools with plants and seeds, and there are various websites (see Taking it further at the end of the chapter) that can be very helpful in setting this up.

Identification of plants and animals

Pupils should be able to

- *identify and name a variety of common animals including fish, amphibians, reptiles, birds and mammals;*

(DfE, 2013, page 148)

- *identify and name a variety of plants and animals in their habitats including micro-habitats.*

(DfE, 2013, page 151)

FACTFILE

A habitat is the area in which a plant or animal lives. Different species often live in the same habitat, for example woodland. A small part of the habitat is called the micro-habitat, eg the area under the stone where the woodlice lives. A community consists of different populations of species living together. In any given habitat there are many different interactions between the organisms in the community and that particular habitat.

Habitats

Pupils should first of all be introduced to the terms habitat and micro-habitat and could undertake some research using books to develop their own knowledge and understanding of plants and animals, first of all in their local area and then in less familiar habitats such as the rainforest. Links could be made to work being done in other subjects such as geography where pupils could compare and contrast the plants and animals in two different countries. They could also do a plant survey of two contrasting sites in the nearby vicinity using a digital camera and talk about similarities and differences. They could visit different habitats and see what happens to the plants and animals in these habitats throughout the different seasons, and how the weather as well as the appearance of the habitat might change. They should be introduced to a variety of fish, amphibians, reptiles, birds and mammals, including those kept as pets.

Pupils should be able to

> *explore and use classification keys to help group, identify and name a variety of living things in their local environment.*

> (DfE, 2013, page 161)

Children in lower Key Stage 2 (Year 4) should be introduced to guides or classification keys and can have a go at identifying plants and animals in their environment which they have observed using these, or try making their own branching key like the one in Figure 4.1.

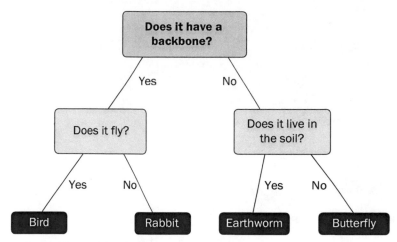

Figure 4.1 *Example of a branching key*

Your pupils could undergo some research into these plants or animals and create their own key with different criteria. Before devising their own keys they will need to list the characteristics which can help divide, for example, a group of plants into flowering plants including grasses and non-flowering plants such as ferns and mosses. This activity can also be done to identify a group of animals using vertebrate animals (those with a backbone) such as fish, amphibians, reptiles, birds and mammals, and invertebrates (those without a backbone) such as snails, slugs, worms, spiders and insects. Children should be encouraged to look at similarities and differences (*working scientifically*). This learning can be further reinforced using computer software for branching keys.

By the end of Year 5 children should be able to explain the differences in the life cycles of a mammal, an amphibian, an insect and a bird and describe the life processes of reproduction in animals. The life cycle of a butterfly is often a popular example. Secondary resources such as books or internet sites (see Taking it further at the end of this chapter) can be of great use here as well as visits to natural history museums and butterfly farms.

By Year 6 pupils should be able to

> describe how living things are classified into broad groups according to common observable characteristics and based on similarities and differences including micro-organisms, plants and animals.

> (DfE, 2013, page 172)

At this point children are building on their knowledge of classification systems learnt in Year 4 and should be introduced to more detailed groupings such as classifying animals into vertebrates, invertebrates and micro-organisms (see Figure 4.2). They could talk about the reasons for assigning an animal to a particular group based on specific characteristics such as whether an animal suckles its young. The children could then find out about the work of Carl Linnaeus, a pioneer of classification, and write an article for a newspaper based on his work.

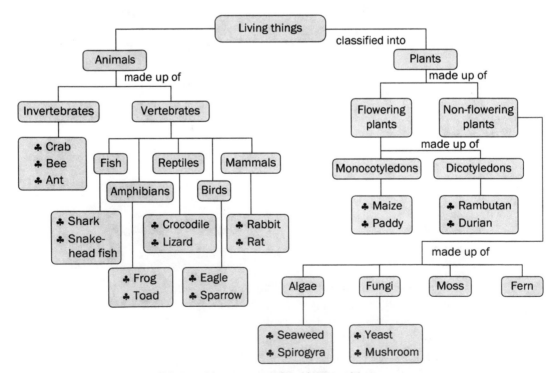

Figure 4.2 *Classification of living things, examples shown with* ♣

FACTFILE

Micro-organisms are very small organisms that can only be seen using a microscope. They belong to various groups such as bacteria, fungi, protozoa and viruses.

Living, non-living and never been alive

Children often have difficulty in identifying things as living, non-living or having never been alive and will often say that anything that moves is alive, including a car. In Year 2 children are required to

> explore and compare the differences between things that are living, dead and things that have never been alive.
>
> (DfE, 2013, page 151)

An interesting activity to do with children using what is familiar to them is to take them on a walk and ask them to identify things that are living, not living and have never been alive. Children could then be asked to work in groups and discuss how an alien would know that a tree is alive but a car is not. You may be surprised by what you hear. Ask them to compare a baby with a car, for example, and prompt them into thinking about how a baby grows and changes. This can then lead you into talking about the properties of life and the idea that all living things have certain characteristics that are essential for keeping them alive and healthy. Pupils should become familiar with the life processes that are common to all living things.

FACTFILE

The seven life processes are movement, respiration, sensitivity, growth, reproduction, excretion and nutrition. An easy way to help children remember these is to use the acronym 'Mrs Gren' and perhaps list the seven life processes with the first letter highlighted to illustrate this.

Habitats, feeding relationships and adaptation

Pupils should be able to:

> -   identify and name a variety of common animals that are carnivores, herbivores and omnivores;
>
> (DfE, 2013, page 148)

> -   identify that most living things live in habitats to which they are suited and describe how different habitats provide for the basic needs of different kinds of animals and plants and how they depend on each other;
>
> (DfE, 2013, page 151)

- *describe how animals obtain their food from plants and other animals, using the idea of a simple food chain, and identify and name different sources of food;*

(DfE, 2013, page 151)

- *construct and interpret a variety of food chains, identifying producers, predators and prey.*

(DfE, 2013, page 162)

Once children are familiar with the term habitat and micro-habitat and can talk about different habitats and micro-habitats in their local area and in less familiar areas, they might predict what plants and animals might be found there. A useful elicitation activity is to introduce a matching game and ask the children to match different animals to their habitats and talk about how those habitats provide for those plants and animals. Young children often think that animals only refer to four-legged animals with fur, and even older children might think that a fish or an insect is not an animal, so be prepared to deal with these misconceptions. They could work in groups to make a list of conditions where certain plants and animals are found, for example woodlice in damp, dark conditions. Be aware that schools often do a topic on mini-beasts and children could for example undergo a mini-beast hunt in two contrasting habitats and list what they have discovered.

FACTFILE

A mini-beast is not a scientific term but one commonly used by teachers and others to refer to a variety of different invertebrates that include, but are not limited to, insects, spiders, worms, slugs, snails and woodlice.

Children might answer questions on a particular mini-beast of their choice, such as:

- where is it found?
- does it have any legs?
- does the body have any segments?
- does it have a soft body or shell?
- is the body divided into regions?

They could be asked to draw or describe their mini-beast, try to identify it and then do some research on what it likes to eat. An investigation could be carried out on whether an earthworm likes the dark or the light (*working scientifically*) where children could be encouraged to predict what they think might happen.

Children might choose an animal and consider how that animal has adapted to their environment. An exciting activity for them to do is to create a fictional creature that has adapted to the environment and list both the environmental conditions such as temperature and rainfall in that particular habitat, and the features that the creature has developed to help it adapt to the habitat. This is a useful assessment exercise.

FACTFILE

A seal has developed whiskers to help it feel fish in the dark, a streamlined body to help it move in the water without resistance and two layers of fur for warmth.

Now you will be in a position to get children to consider the interdependence of living things in a particular habitat and think about what they eat to help them survive. The following elicitation activity will help you to assess children's understanding of the following ecological terms and their knowledge of feeding relationships.

Elicitation

A concept map includes items enclosed in a circle with the relationship between these things shown by a connecting line. Figure 4.3 shows a concept map about food chains. An incomplete version of this concept map can be used to assess pupils' understanding. Alternatively, provide the children with the terms **plants**, **carnivores**, **herbivores**, **consumers**, **producers** and **habitats** and ask them to join the words to illustrate the relationship between them. Children need practice in completing concept maps so it is always a good idea to start with a few on topics that are more familiar to the children, eg a TV programme, before embarking on a scientific one.

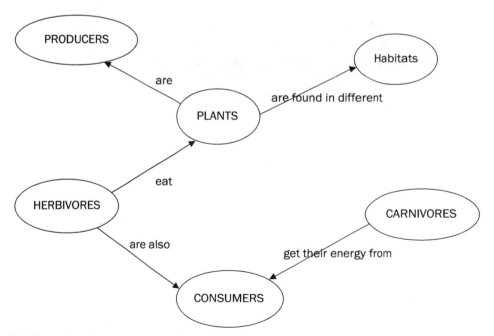

Figure 4.3 *Completed concept map for a food chain*

FACTFILE

A food chain or web is used to illustrate the feeding relationships among organisms, as shown in Figure 4.4. It usually starts with the Sun as the energy source, then green plants and ends with a species that is not eaten by other species. A food chain describes the transfer of energy through an ecosystem with the arrows showing the direction of flow of energy. There are rarely more than five living things in a food chain. Note that with young children it is common to describe food chains as starting with a green plant rather than the Sun, due to their difficulty in understanding the idea of photosynthesis.

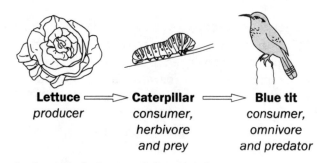

Lettuce ⟹ **Caterpillar** ⟹ **Blue tit**
producer   *consumer,*   *consumer,*
               herbivore   *omnivore*
               and prey   *and predator*

Figure 4.4 *Example of a food chain (arrows left to right)*

It is essential to stress the importance of the arrow and the direction of the flow of energy, ie who is eating what. This can be reinforced with Figure 4.5 where the arrows go from right to left but the food chain still begins with the producer and ends with the predator.

Fox   ⟸   Rabbit   ⟸   Carrot

Figure 4.5 *Example of a food chain (arrows right to left)*

A natural progression would be to take children on a walk of the school grounds to see whether they can find evidence of any food chains in their local environment, for example nibbled leaves. The children could then illustrate their own food chains in different habitats using pictures and arrows. It is important for children to realise that we also depend on plants and animals for our food, so ask the children to look at the contents of their lunch boxes and see whether they can trace the sources of the food.

Food Chain game

Knowledge of food chains can be made memorable by playing the Food Chain game.

Give each child one of the following labels for each of the habitats:

- *Woodland habitat*: woodland plant, woodlice, blue tit, hawk
- *Pond habitat*: algae, worm, great diving beetle, frog, heron
- *Garden habitat*: dead leaves, fungi and bacteria, mite, ant, centipede, hedgehog, fox
- *Sea habitat*: plankton, fish, penguin, killer whale
- *Urban habitat*: leaves, grasshopper, chicken, human

The labels are the names of organisms of different food chains found in different habitats. It is important to have one food chain where you can illustrate that a human is part of the food chain too. Ask the children to move around the room and see whether they can arrange themselves in their particular food chain showing what eats what. It is a good idea to colour co-ordinate the labels for the food chains in each habitat to make the task more manageable.

Less able children can be given food chains for habitats with which they are more familiar or those which have fewer feeding (trophic) levels. Children with special needs can access the same activity by using pictures instead of labels with words. The more able can be extended by being given more challenging examples such as a food chain including algae or one with more trophic levels. It is important for children to understand that humans and animals ultimately depend on green plants for their survival and if something happens to the green plant it will affect everything else in the food chain.

FACTFILE

Only a small amount of energy from the Sun is converted into chemical energy by the plant as most of it is reflected, and much of the energy obtained from plants by consumers such as caterpillars is used to maintain their life processes. It is estimated that about 90% of the energy is lost at each link of the food chain.

An extension activity with a very able class might illustrate how inefficient the flow of energy is in a food chain. Ask children with the labels representing one of the simpler food chains, for example the urban habitat shown above, to come to the front of the class. Hold a big sheet of A3 paper and tell them that you are the Sun and you have all this energy to give to the plant but most of it is going to be wasted and only a small proportion is to be used by the plant. Ask the child representing the plant to rip the paper in half and throw the other half away. Then they pass the half of the A3 sheet to the grasshopper and the same thing happens so only half of that piece of paper passes on as energy to the chicken and then the same happens with the chicken, so only a small proportion of the energy eventually reaches the human. It is difficult to explain the idea of only 10% of energy being passed and used at each level of the food chain with young children, but the idea of inefficiency of energy transfer can be illustrated just as well by ripping the paper in half.

Playing games with children is a fun way of reinforcing scientific concepts that might otherwise be difficult to understand. Playing the Woolly Worm game can get children to understand predator–prey relationships in a food chain and provides an appreciation of the idea of competition for resources. Cut out lengths of string or coloured wool and spread them out on the school field. Tell the children that they are blue tits and need to collect three bits of wool representing worms and bring them to you every time you blow the whistle – if not they are out of the game. As the game progresses it will be harder and harder to find the bits of wool thus illustrating the idea of resources being scarce. An extra dimension can be added to the game by asking two or three children to be eagles (predators) that prey on the blue tits (prey) to show predator and prey relationships.

Human impact on the environment

Pupils should be able to

> recognise that environments can change and this can sometimes pose dangers to living things.
>
> (DfE, 2013, page 161)

The new national curriculum (DfE, 2013) suggests that pupils should explore examples of both positive and negative human impacts on the environment. Children could come up with a list of the positive effects of a local nature reserve, for example, or design a poster illustrating the negative effects of litter. Older children could debate the pros and cons of deforestation. It is important for children to appreciate the changes that are occurring in their local area as well as changes further afield.

A concept cartoon (Keogh and Naylor, 2000) is an effective way of asking children to consider different points of view. It is a cartoon-style drawing showing different characters debating an everyday occurrence which may not have a single right answer. Its aim is to promote discussion and stimulate thinking.

Plants

Conditions of growth

Pupils should be able to:

- *observe and describe how seeds and bulbs grow into mature plants;*
- *find out and describe how plants need water, light and a suitable temperature to grow and stay healthy.*

> (DfE, 2013, page 152)

Children have many misconceptions about germination and the conditions of growth of plants which need to be addressed when teaching this topic.

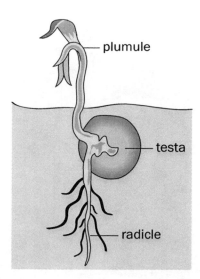

Figure 4.6 A germinating seed

FACTFILE

The conditions required for a seed to germinate are different from the conditions needed for plants to grow. A seed needs water, oxygen and a suitable temperature to germinate. It does not need soil or light. The seed absorbs the water and its embryo swells and splits the testa; the radicle appears and grows downwards and the plumule grows upwards (see Figure 4.6).

A plant, however, needs water, oxygen and light energy from the Sun so that it can produce its own food through photosynthesis. A bulb is an underground root structure that holds the complete life cycle of a plant and has a store of food. A fruit is the mature ovary of a flowering plant that is edible and usually eaten raw.

An effective way of starting your teaching is to show a collection of fruits of different colours and shapes. Children can make some observational drawings and this can be followed by cutting open the fruit to expose its different parts. Alternatively children can be given different plants and seeds and asked to guess where the seeds came from so that they can appreciate that seeds are part of the fruit and the fruit is part of the plant. They could be asked to consider whether the largest seed grows into the tallest plant, thus asking them to look for patterns and relationships (*working scientifically*). Children could plant a variety of seeds so they can observe them germinating. Broad beans in plastic lemonade bottles as seen in Figure 4.7 are very effective in demonstrating the root and shoot starting to grow.

Try germinating seeds other than cress, which is commonly used in primary schools, and germinate seeds in interesting places, eg wellies. Children can draw pictures of the seed germinating or write a diary describing the changes taking place. The same can be done with bulbs, eg daffodils, and children can observe and record in a table the growth of the plant as it changes over time (*working scientifically*). Alternative tasks are to ask them to observe

Figure 4.7 *Broad bean germinating in a bottle*

similar plants at different stages of growth or use time lapse videos to show how plants move and grow.

By the end of Year 3 pupils should be able to

> *explore the requirements of plants for life and growth (air, water, nutrients from the soil and room to grow) and how they vary from plant to plant.*
>
> (DfE, 2013, page 157)

In Year 2 children will have been introduced to the requirements of plants for growth and survival, such as light and water. They might have covered a leaf on a plant with black sugar paper for a period of time and then taken the paper off and noted how the leaf has gone yellow because of lack of light. This activity is better than killing a whole plant to illustrate this point. In Year 3 they could carry out tests to determine the effect of different factors, such as the amount of fertiliser or water, on plant growth (*working scientifically*). Bring in a collection of labels from garden and house plants which will illustrate the needs of the plant. Ask the children to think about how animals obtain their food for growth and discuss the differences between plants and animals. Note that according to the new national curriculum

> *pupils can be introduced to the idea that plants can make their own food but at this stage do not need to understand how it happens.*
>
> (DfE, 2013, page 151)

Functions of different parts of the plant

Pupils should be able to:

- *identify and describe the functions of different parts of flowering plants, roots, stem/trunk, leaves and flowers;*

- *investigate the way in which water is transported within plants.*

> (DfE, 2013, page 157)

Children should learn about the structure and function of the different parts of a plant. They could first of all draw a diagram labelling and learning the names of the different parts, perhaps using interactive whiteboard resources as reinforcement in the plenary of lessons, before learning about the functions of these parts. Be ready to tackle misconceptions such as plants get food from the soil through their roots and the function of the stem is to carry food to the flower. A popular activity undertaken in school to illustrate how water is transported in plants is to place white carnations or celery in coloured water and observe how water travels up the stem (if using the latter keep the leaves and cut up the celery after and place under a digital microscope). The leaves will turn the colour of the water and show how the water has been transported up the plant. The digital microscope will enable you to see the coloured dye in the actual celery. Children can look at the roots of a variety of plants with different root systems, for example tap roots, and examine and draw the roots talking about their colour and shape. They could make a model of the different root systems using straws and pipe cleaners.

FACTFILE

The root system of a plant is needed for support as well as absorbing water and mineral salts from the soil and passing them into the stem. The upward passage of water from the soil is known as transpiration. Fibrous roots grow in plants where there is no distinguishable main root and several roots grow out at the same time, as in grasses and cereals. Adventitious roots are those that grow not from a main root but directly from the stem, as in bulbs and corms. A tap root grows vertically into the soil and later lateral roots grow from this at an acute angle outwards and downwards, and from these laterals other branches may arise. The stem holds the plant upright and spreads out leaves for photosynthesis. The principal role of the leaf is to manufacture food through photosynthesis (where carbon dioxide and water are combined using the energy from the Sun to produce sugar and oxygen).

Life cycle of plants

Pupils should be able to:

- *explore the part that flowers play in the life cycle of flowering plants including pollination, seed formation and seed dispersal;*

    (DfE, 2013, page 157)

- *describe the life processes of reproduction in some plants.*

    (DfE, 2013, page 168)

A variety of visual, practical activities can be used to teach children about the life cycles of plants in a fun and interesting way. They primarily need to understand that the flower is responsible for reproduction and seed dispersal.

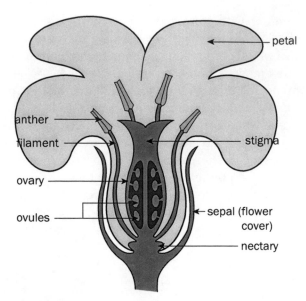

Figure 4.8 *Main parts of a flower*

FACTFILE

Figure 4.8 shows the main parts of a flower. The five stages of the sexual reproductive cycle of a flowering plant are:

1.   pollination;

2.   fertilisation;

3.   seed formation;

4.   seed dispersal;

5.   germination.

Pollination takes place when pollen from an anther is carried to a stigma. In self-pollination, pollen is carried to the stigma of the same plant. Cross-pollination occurs when pollen is carried to the stigma of another plant through insect or wind pollination. Pollen grains, for example, will adhere to the bodies of bees and allow them to move pollen from one plant to another.

Seed dispersal is the movement of seeds away from the parent plant. Seeds can be dispersed by the plant itself through the effect of gravity on heavier fruits causing them to fall from the plant when ripe, eg apples. Seeds can be dispersed by wind when they float in the breeze or flutter to the ground, such as with dandelions which have feathery bristles attached to their seeds and can be dispersed a long distance. Seeds can also be dispersed by animals by being transported externally on the outside of vertebrate animals or through ingestion.

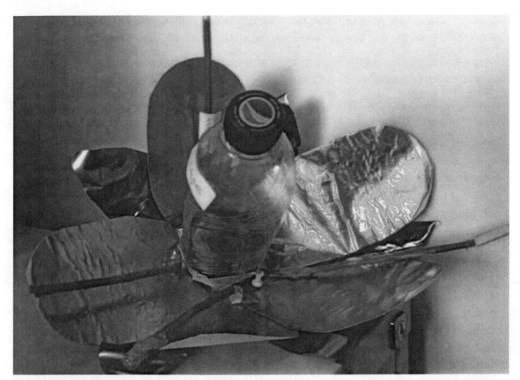

Figure 4.9 *A model of a flowering plant*

Some plants, however, reproduce by asexual (vegetative) reproduction, where parts of the parent plant separate to form new plants which are exactly the same as the parent, for example strawberry plants sending out runners, or potato tubers.

The following activities could be carried out.

• Children could look at the inside of real flowers, eg tulips, to identify the different parts. They could make a model of a flowering plant using a small lemonade bottle, pipe cleaners and card (see Figure 4.9) which would be a useful assessment exercise.

• They could discuss why some petals are brightly coloured and why insects are attracted to certain flowers. Children could use a digital microscope to magnify plants and leaves and pollen in the stamen.

• They could role play pollination by using polystyrene balls on sticks, with the balls representing the pollen grains that can be transferred between the anthers in flowers to stigmas by butterflies, being represented by other children.

• They could look at fruits with different seeds and discuss in groups how they might have been dispersed. They could look at the fruits of the sycamore tree and the various parts of the seed inside the hard case of the fruit, for example, and compare how the seed falls through the air with other winged seeds. They could explore how many puffs of air it takes to release the seeds from a dandelion clock.

- Older children might try growing new plants from different parts of the parent plant, eg root cuttings, tubers and bulbs.

- Children could compare the life cycles of plants in their local environment with those in other parts of the world, for example desert areas, or even those from prehistoric times.

CROSS-CURRICULAR LINKS

There are many opportunities to promote cross-curricular links with this scientific focus, while also promoting literacy and numeracy. You can try out the following ideas when studying this subject.

Literacy

Literacy can be promoted by asking children to keep a diary of what they see in their garden or school field over the course of a week, or they could write a letter to the local council opposing a change to a given habitat. Children can use books to undergo research into famous naturalists such as David Attenborough and could write a biography of his life. Alternatively they can design an information sheet giving details of the plants and animals found in their environment. Younger children will enjoy *Monkey Puzzle* by Julia Donaldson and Axel Scheffler which can be used when teaching children about the life cycles of animals.

Numeracy

Numeracy can be promoted by asking young children to compare different seeds and sort them according to the longest/shortest or thinnest/fattest. They could collect data on the rate of growth of different shoots and roots and record it in a table and then draw a graph. Alternatively they could use an ICT database to interrogate the information held about plants or animals. They could use tables to record the number of different plants and animals found in their local area and then create bar charts.

Other curricular links

Plants, habitats and living things has strong links with other subjects in the primary curriculum. In geography they could compare two habitats in two contrasting localities, for example contrasting the UK with a tropical country such as Jamaica. They could find out in which countries different animals live and plot these on a map of the world. In design and technology pupils could design and make a worm farm as they learn about animals in their local environment. How human beings have used plants for food or medicine throughout the ages could be explored in history.

HEALTH AND SAFETY

Be Safe in Science (ASE, 2010) provides some useful information on things to take into consideration when teaching this topic and is a good source of reference. Remember, for example, to:

- undergo a risk assessment of the local environment when taking children out;

- ensure all offsite visits follow LEA/school guidelines;

- ask children to wash hands after handling soil or plants and animals;

- teach children to avoid touching eyes while handling plants and to never taste any part of the plant unless certain that it is safe to do so;

- consider the likelihood of contamination of soil samples;

- consider the need for wearing gloves;

- avoid substances to which children may be allergic, such as fruits and seeds, and especially peanuts;

- avoid poisonous plants: red kidney beans (before cooking), holly, tomato leaves, rhubarb leaves, potato leaves, mountain ash seeds;

- ensure children do not handle plant fertiliser;

- avoid keeping animals that can transmit diseases to humans, those that are illegal, venomous, or those that may infest or cause allergic reactions.

Critical questions

» *Identify the specific areas of the topic where you feel less confident in your subject knowledge.*

» *What else might you do to develop your subject knowledge in these areas?*

» *Consider how you would use the outside environment in your school to teach children this topic.*

Taking it further

DfE (2006) *Learning Outside the Classroom Manifesto*. London: DfE Publications.

Hoath, L (2008) *Teaching Life Processes*. *Primary Science Review*, PSR 101.

Jewell, N (2002) *What's Inside a Seed*. *Primary Science Review*, PSR 75.

Russell, T and Watt, D (1990) *Growth, SPACE Research Report*. Liverpool: Liverpool University Press.

Websites

www.bbc.co.uk/nature/animals/planetearth/hd

www.earthrestorationservice.org/

www.edenproject.com/

www.growingschools.org.uk/

www.keepbritaintidy.org/EcoSchools?gclid=CJD8s8W1w7kCFc5V3godtn4Axw

www.kew.org/

www.kids.nationalgeographic.com/kids/

www.naturalhistorymuseum.org.uk

www.rospa.com

www.wildlifetrusts.org/

References

ASE (2010) *Be Safe in Science*. Hatfield: ASE.

DfE (2013) *Teachers' Standards*. www.gov.uk/government/uploads/system/uploads/attachment_data/file/208682/Teachers__Standards_2013.pdf (accessed 17 February 2014).

Keogh, B and Naylor, S (2000) *Concept Cartoons in KS2 Science Education*. Sandbach: Millgate House Publishers.

5 Evolution and inheritance

Introduction

Children from an early age will learn about the variety of life on Earth and where it can be found. As they develop they will soon start to recognise and acknowledge how some animals are different, from the giraffe with its long neck to the polar bear with its white fur. They will also start to realise that living things are adapted to their immediate environments and without such adaptations they would soon fail to flourish and may even perish. Pupils can find evidence of changes to plants and animals not only in the fauna and flora of today but also through the evidence of the fossil record. Children will also become aware of how living things depend on each other for food or shelter.

As children get older they will become more aware that characteristics of living things are passed from the parents to their offspring and pupils begin to appreciate that variation in the young over time can make animals more or less able to survive in particular environments. For the first time in the new national curriculum (DfE, 2013) evolution and inheritance have become a real focus of pupils' study.

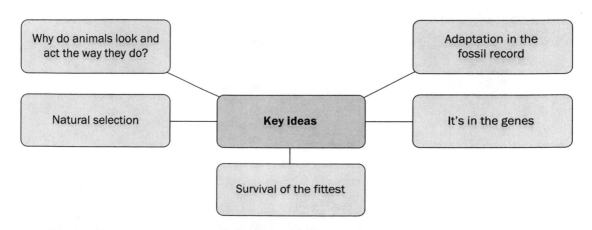

KEY VOCABULARY

The new national curriculum (DfE, 2013) stresses the importance of children using technical terminology accurately and precisely and building up an extended specialist vocabulary.

In Key Stage 1, though pupils will not directly have to study the key factors that control the evolution and inheritance of living things, they will have begun to explore the basic vocabulary to describe how living things are suited to their **habitats** and **micro-habitats**, for example on the **seashore**, in **woodland**, **oceans** and **rainforests**.

In upper Key Stage 2, in Year 6 you should continue to develop pupils' vocabulary linked specifically to **evolution** and **inheritance**. Pupils should learn that living things produce similar **offspring** which sometimes vary to produce a **hybrid**, and offspring may not be exactly identical to their parents. The children must also recognise that animals and plants are **adapted** to suit their environment in a variety of ways and that adaptation can lead to **evolution, natural variation, natural selection** and **survival of the fittest**. These natural variations are stored within our **genes** and our **chromosomes**, which provide a blueprint for life on Earth.

CHILDREN'S IDEAS AND COMMON MISCONCEPTIONS

During the study of this topic children may hold various misconceptions about how animals and humans have evolved and adapted over time. At an early age these may consist of the following:

- animals and plants are just made the way they are for no particular reason;
- animals and plants do not share a common origin.

Further misconceptions that may become apparent as children learn more about the topic are that:

- fossils are not part of evolutionary development;
- the fossil record is somehow disconnected from the plants and creatures found today;
- plants and animals do not develop natural variations over time.

Topics and teaching strategies

Why do animals look and act the way they do?

Young children will have noticed the variety of animals and plants that inhabit not only their immediate environment but also the wider world. They should be able to name a variety of large and small animals such as the elephant, giraffe and tarantula; however they also need to be made aware that these animals have evolved and have adapted to survive and flourish in the habitats in which they now live. As the new curriculum states, Year 2 pupils need to be able to

> *identify that most living things live in habitats to which they are suited.*
>
> (DfE, 2013, page 151)

By looking at living creatures, where they live and what they eat, you can start to introduce children to the idea, linked to evolution, that creatures live and thrive in the environments that best suit them. These may be seen in terms of habitats or micro-habitats.

It is important that children understand that living things have specially adapted over time to meet the conditions in which they now find themselves. It is important that children recognise the variety of creatures and plants that may be found within any one species and that this variety of life has a common origin.

You can start to explore these ideas by providing children with pictures or videos of well-known creatures such as polar bears, camels, penguins and giraffes. Ask them where they live and what they eat. As you talk to pupils start to explore the characteristics of these creatures and find out if the children realise that their physical characteristics are linked to where they live. For example, the giraffe's long neck helps it reach the very high leaves on the trees in Africa that other animals cannot reach and their dextrous tongues can extract leaves from the thorniest of branches. Ask the children if they think these creatures always looked like this in order to assess their understanding of how these animals may have changed over time to suit their environments. Pupils should begin to be aware of the relationships between different groups of animals, for example that polar bears are related to other bears such as brown bears even though they live in very different environments. Challenge pupils to consider why this is. This can be developed in upper Key Stage 2 by considering the range of creatures that can be found preserved within the fossil record (see also Chapter 8).

Adaptation in the fossil record

In upper Key Stage 2 children will need to

> *recognise that living things have changed over time and that fossils provide information about living things that inhabited the Earth millions of years ago.*
>
> (DfE, 2013, page 173)

FACTFILE

Trilobites were creatures which lived on the floor of Earth's ancient oceans. They ate both algae and small organisms and were armoured sea creatures that looked similar to giant woodlice. These sea creatures were arthropods which had around 15,000 different species types and ranged in size from millimetres to tens of centimetres. They existed in the Palaeozoic period, from about 542 million to 251 million years ago.

Archaeopteryx is believed to be the earliest known bird. It had bird-like features such as a beak and feet. It evolved from dinosaurs such as raptors and had fingers, claws and teeth which showed this early evolutionary link. It is believed it could fly; however, it seemed to have spent much of its time on the ground and flying only short distances.

By getting children to examine the fossil record they will begin to realise how varied life on Earth has been in the past and how much, or how little, organisms have changed over time. They will start to realise that certain species have evolved and changed to survive the environments in which they lived. However, it is important that you tell the children that the fossil record is in fact incomplete and therefore there are gaps because not all living things have been fossilised well, tectonic movements over time may have destroyed evidence or they simply have yet to be discovered.

One creature that is well worth getting children to observe (*working scientifically*) and draw is the trilobite. Since it lived over quite a long geological period you can see how it evolved over time and you can draw such changes to the attention of pupils. By selecting a variety of trilobite images to show pupils you get children to see how trilobites' eyes varied greatly over their reign on Earth.

Trilobites were one of the first creatures to evolve simple compound eyes, much like insects today. You can ask the children why they think trilobites needed better eyes. Some trilobites had no eyes; again ask them why. Some children will suggest they had not yet evolved but the reason for this is that some trilobites lived deep in the dark oceans where no light was present and hence eyes were not useful to them. Other trilobites had eyes so large that they dominated the top part of their body. Again ask them to consider why. What advantage (such as providing a 360-degree visual field to protect them from their enemies) might it have given them?

You can also use specific images of fossils such as the Archaeopteryx. By showing pupils its bird-like features and contrasting these with its dinosaur features you will be able to open up a discussion with the children about this early evolutionary link.

Similarly, one of the few animals for which we have a fairly complete evolutionary record is the horse. By studying examples of primitive horses you will be able to show how features such as their multi-toed feet evolved into what we see today as single-toed hooves, which have adapted to help them run more easily.

You can use the work of palaeontologist Mary Anning (see Chapter 8) to show the importance of the fossil record in our understanding of the development of life on our planet over geological time.

Natural selection

As well as studying the fossil record pupils in Year 6 must

> *identify how animals and plants are adapted to suit their environment in different ways and that adaptation may lead to evolution.*
>
> (DfE, 2013, page 173)

During their study of rocks, discussed in Chapter 8, children will have come across the work of Charles Darwin, the English naturalist who in 1859 in his *Origin of Species* proposed that the pattern of evolution was a result of what he termed natural selection. This meant creatures refined their existence over time due to their circumstances to best meet their survival needs. Pupils may have also come across other important figures in this field such as Alfred Wallace. It is now important to draw meaningful modern day concrete links between what hitherto have been seen as the evolution of life only found in ancient creatures.

Ask children to collect pictures or to carry out research using secondary sources into creatures that they recognise as having particular features pertinent to their species, such as the giraffe with its long neck or the webbed feet and spoon-like bill of the duck. Ask the children to think about why these animals have such features and if they have always looked that way. This exercise will allow children to start considering the idea of adaptation within species and how it may have benefited them.

By observing (*working scientifically*) and focusing on the variety of birds in the school grounds and children's immediate environment you will be able to give children a first-hand insight into how birds' beaks have adapted to suit a variety of tasks and food sources. Supplement these observations with photographs of less common species of birds such as golden eagles and parrots. Figure 5.1 illustrates a variety of beak types which you can use to get children to guess what each sort of bird eats.

Heron   Sparrow-hawk   Duck

Figure 5.1 *Beak types*

Get children to look at birds that have beaks to chisel with such as a woodpecker, beaks to tear meat such as the sparrow-hawk and eagle, beaks or bills that strain plants and animals out of water such as ducks, probing beaks to get nectar out of flowers such as humming birds, spear-like beaks for catching fish such as the heron and kingfisher and beaks for cracking seeds such as finches and parrots. You could ask children to consider would birds with chisel-like beaks be any good at trying to eat seeds, and if not why not. Ask them to think what would happen if these two species lived together in a similar habitat. Which would thrive and why? Would one species diminish and die out if they could not adapt?

Following on from this you can get children to think about how some animals have used adaptation in the form of camouflage to survive in a range of habitats such as jungles and grassy plains. Examine pictures of moths and butterflies or larger creatures such as zebras and tigers in order to explore this.

A practical means of developing this concept is to ask children to cut out small identical fish shapes, about 6cm wide, from different types of paper (use scissors, newspaper and large sheets of coloured sugar paper). Then get them to put several large sheets of A2 newspaper out on their tables and to spread their range of fish randomly out on it. Then tell the children to individually act like feeding sharks or tuna and to quickly try and pick up the fish that can be easily seen and to put them into piles on another table once they have been collected.

Ask the children to count the range of fish collected after 1 minute of 'feeding'. Get them to compare the coloured sugar-paper fish they have picked up with the newspaper fish. Did they pick up more of one type? If so, get them to consider why. Children will quickly realise that the newspaper fish were less obvious when laid on the newspaper and will be able to link this learning to the idea of how camouflage works and the advantage it gives to living creatures. This idea can then be used to consider with the children what would happen if the remaining fish left by the shark were of one particular type, as with the newspaper fish. How might this affect the future development or evolution of the various types of fish in these investigations? You will be able to suggest to pupils that the newspaper fish have an evolutionary advantage over the other types which could help them flourish, and that over time the less adapted species would diminish and die out. This links nicely to the notion of the survival of the fittest.

Survival of the fittest

It is worth considering with pupils the fact that evolutionary change happens over many generations of species. Explain that this is why it is hard to see the adaptation and evolution of species around today. When children look in the mirror they see no change but they are in fact changing slightly every time they look. Similarly, evolutionary changes in plant and animal species are slow but it does not mean they are not happening. You can link this back to the fossil record where the vast amounts of geological time help you to see such evolutionary changes more easily.

FACTFILE

The Cretaceous period was about 145 million years ago and saw a period of mass extinction, most noticeably the death of the dinosaurs. However, many other organisms died at the end of this period including the ammonites. This mass extinction has been attributed to a catastrophic comet or asteroid strike near Mexico which led to a change in the Earth's climate.

The dodo is an extinct flightless bird that lived on Mauritius in the Indian Ocean. It was approximately 1m tall and weighed around 15kg. It had brownish-grey plumage, a naked head and a black, yellow and green beak. It is believed that increased competition from non-indigenous humans on their land, hunting and animals brought by settlers may have led to its ultimate extinction.

The emperor penguin is the largest of 17 species of penguin. It is approximately 1.15m tall and it inhabits the open ice of the Antarctic during the winter. They have strong claws on their feet which help them to grip on to the surface of the ice and snow and they may often be seen to slide on their bellies to move around more quickly.

Explore with children what will happen to animals or plants if they cannot adapt quickly enough to change in their environment. This could provide a good starting point for learning about the mass extinction of the dinosaurs in the Cretaceous period or the demise of the dodo.

You can also get children to consider how developments in animal behaviour also provide creatures with an evolutionary advantage to survive in a variety of environments. For example, emperor penguins huddle together and take small steps every 30–60 seconds, which leads to large-scale reorganisation of the huddle over time. This helps to keep them warm and save energy in the 110mph driving winds and the 45°C cold of the Antarctic.

To investigate this notion get children to fill small lemonade bottles with warm water and ask them to record the temperature of one bottle, using data loggers (*working scientifically*), if it is left outside in a cool breeze on its own. Ask them to record how quickly the temperature of the bottle goes down. Now ask them to repeat this experiment with 10 bottles in a huddle. What happens to the temperature of the bottles on the outside if they are left there all the time? Then get children to compare a bottle's temperature if it is moved throughout the huddle.

Other behaviours may also be examined to reinforce this evolutionary benefit of changing behaviour. An example is the emperor penguin holding its solitary egg on its feet off the ground and covering it with a warm layer of feathered skin called a brood pouch.

It's in the genes

The new curriculum (DfE, 2013) suggests that children in Year 6 should

> recognise that living things produce offspring of the same kind, but normally offspring vary and are not identical to their parents.
>
> (DfE, 2013, page 173)

Children should be introduced to the idea that characteristics of animals are passed from parents to their offspring. While it is not statutory for them to understand the idea of genes and chromosomes it may be helpful to use this terminology along with some basic explanations.

FACTFILE

Genes are sets of chemical instructions found within every cell of each living plant or animal. They provide the instructions or blueprints for creating new living things. Genes are joined together into long strands of material called deoxyribonucleic acid (DNA) and these bundles of genes are known as chromosomes. During sexual reproduction half of a person's genes come from the mother while the other half come from the father. These genes combine to give that human its individuality.

To help children understand that the parent of a living thing passes on their characteristics in their genes it is worth getting children to look at images of the royal family and compare them against images of their offspring, such as the Queen and Prince Charles. You could also get them to look at their own grandparents to see if they can spot any similarities.

For children who own and know about dogs it is worth extending this discussion to the breeds of dogs and their characteristics. By doing this children will no doubt end up talking about cross-breeds or mongrels and how they are a mix of two types of dog. Encourage pupils to think about and to describe characteristics that have been passed down from the parent. Ask them what makes it identifiable as a mongrel rather than a purebred pedigree. You should ask them *If these two animals were to breed together again would it give exactly the same animal?* You need to get children to realise that there is a degree of random chance as to how these animals will gain characteristics so therefore no two animals are likely to be identical, unless they are identical twins.

It can be fun to talk about unusual mixes of animals or hybrids such as a tigon which is the offspring of a tiger and a lion. Explore possible combinations of hybrid creatures by giving them a bag of laminated pictures of the pieces of two distinct but somewhat similar animals such as a donkey and a zebra. Give them items such as the tail, torso, legs, feet, eyes, ears and face shape and see what random hybrid creatures they can create.

You can also talk to children about the idea of how you might improve a breed by selectively breeding in characteristics or developing plants so that they give a higher yield of crops. It is possible to extend this conversation into the ethical issues that this might bring up and whether it is right to mess with Mother Nature's creations. Though it is not statutory, more able children could debate the benefits and drawbacks of genetic engineering and how we can now manipulate DNA to produce changes in living things.

CROSS-CURRICULAR LINKS

There are many opportunities to promote cross-curricular links with this scientific focus while also promoting literacy and numeracy. You can try out the following ideas when studying this subject.

Literacy

Literacy can be promoted by writing some descriptive pieces of work telling the stories of how creatures such as the duck-billed platypus got its characteristics, like the creatures and stories invented by Rudyard Kipling in his *Just So Stories*. You can also develop pupils' non-fiction writing by building up factfiles about the animals or plants that they have studied. The children could be encouraged to write some poems to capture the movements and feelings of some of the more iconic of the many living creatures studied such as the giraffe and the rattlesnake.

Numeracy

Numeracy can be promoted by looking at the temperature scale and measurements associated with living things. They could create comparative graphs of the number of living creatures found on the various continents around the world. They could also be introduced to the early stages of probability and how likely it is that a creature might survive.

Other curricular links

This aspect of study can be used to examine the geographical range of habitats in which creatures can be found around our Earth. You could also encourage children to visit museums to look at ancient remains, such as dinosaur skeletons, to see how the species that have inherited our Earth have change over time. This focus of study can provide you with opportunities to build shelters for humans to survive in the extreme environments that animals can be found in. You can encourage children during art to paint images of ancient creatures in the form of cave art or even consider the camouflage needed to hide dinosaurs from their predators. By asking children to listen to music such as the *Carnival of the Animals* by Camille Saint-Saens they will be able to see how music can be used to conjure up images of the movement of a variety of animals.

HEALTH AND SAFETY

Remember when studying this topic to warn children that

- as with other topics, if handling creatures or plants be aware of the need to wash hands thoroughly before and after contact with them.

Critical questions

» *On a scale of 1–10 (with 10 being completely confident) how confident do you now feel in your own subject knowledge of evolution and inheritance as a topic?*

» *Identify the specific areas where you feel less confident.*

» *Where else might you look and what else might you do to develop your subject knowledge in those areas?*

» *What resources do you need to collect in order to successfully start teaching this topic?*

» *Do you need to collect a bank of photographs of creatures that show variations due to the habitat in which they live?*

Taking it further

Books

Carle, E (1988) *The Mixed-up Chameleon*. London: Puffin Books.

Donaldson, J (2009) *Monkey Puzzle Jigsaw Book*. London: Macmillan Publishers.

Hopkinson, D (2010) *The Humblebee Hunter, Hyperion – Charles Darwin and His Children Investigate Bees*. New York: Disney Hyperion.

Jenkins, M (2008) *The Emperor's Egg*. London: Walker Books.

Swinburne, S and Peterson, M (2010) *Ocean Soup: Tide Pool Poems*, Watertown, MA: Charlesbridge.

Websites

www.bbc.co.uk/nature/life/Trilobite (accessed 2 February 2014).

www.bbc.co.uk/sn/prehistoric_life/human/human_evolution (accessed 2 February 2014).

www.bbc.co.uk/programmes/b00sy534/clips (accessed 2 February 2014).

http://darwin200.christs.cam.ac.uk/pages/index.php?page_id=j (accessed 2 February 2014).

www.trilobites.info/ (accessed 2 February 2014).

References

DfE (2013) *Teachers' Standards*. www.gov.uk/government/uploads/system/uploads/attachment_data/file/208682/Teachers__Standards_2013.pdf (accessed 17 February 2014).

6 Everyday materials and their properties

Introduction

Materials and their properties is a topic which helps children understand the world around them, as everything is made up of materials or substances. Children are exposed to different materials from the time they are born and the topic provides lots of opportunities for exploration and play, especially with very young children. It is an exciting topic to teach as there are lots of opportunities for practical, hands-on activities which can result in the development of scientific skills such as observation, sorting, classifying and questioning. The study of materials is fundamental to understanding many aspects of science such as forces or light. It is, however, a broad topic which involves some complex scientific ideas, so it is important that you as a teacher understand these ideas and the definitions of the many terms associated with the topic. You will find that children will associate the term 'material' with its everyday meaning and will often think that material simply refers to fabrics. It is thus vital that they first of all develop a scientific understanding of the term and appreciate that everything around us is made up of materials or substances that can be classified in different ways, according to their type, origin, properties or uses.

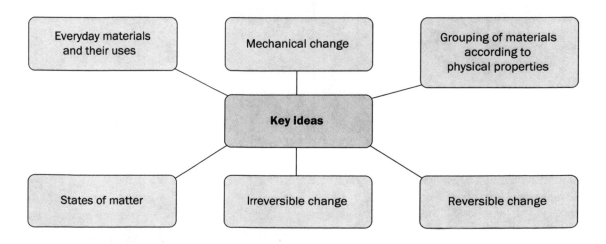

KEY VOCABULARY

The new national curriculum (DfE, 2013) stresses the importance of children using technical terminology accurately and precisely and building up an extended specialist vocabulary.

In Key Stage 1 children should become familiar with the names of everyday materials such as **wood**, **paper**, **cardboard**, **plastic**, **glass**, **metal**, **brick**, **elastic** or **foil** and learn basic vocabulary to describe everyday materials and their simple physical properties, such as **hard/soft**, **stretchy/stiff**, **shiny/dull**, **rough/smooth**, **bendy/not bendy**, **waterproof/not waterproof**, **absorbent/not absorbent** and **opaque/transparent**. During Years 1 and 2, children should also become familiar with vocabulary associated with changing materials such as **squashing**, **bending**, **twisting** and **stretching**. In Years 4 and 5 they should be introduced to vocabulary linked to the states of matter such as **solid**, **liquid** or **gas**, **Celsius**, **melting**, **solidifying**, **evaporation** and **condensation** which can be linked to their knowledge of the **water cycle**. As children develop a more systematic understanding of materials and their properties, they should use vocabulary such as **solubility**, **transparency** and **conductivity** (electrical and thermal). They will use terms such as **dissolve**, **solution** and **substance** and vocabulary associated with separating **mixtures** such as **filtering** and **sieving**. They will also need to understand the terms **reversible** and **irreversible change** and processes such as **burning** and **rusting**.

CHILDREN'S IDEAS AND COMMON MISCONCEPTIONS

During the study of this topic, children may hold various misconceptions about materials and their properties. The term man-made, for example, causes a great deal of confusion because if the object under discussion is not found in nature in that form, for example a wooden peg, then children often believe a human must have made it. At an early age they may think that:

- the term material only applies to solids, so a gas is not a material;
- solids are hard and heavy and liquids are always heavier than gases;
- a powder is a liquid;
- all gases are poisonous;
- only ice melts, not other substances;
- water in a puddle disappears.

As children get older and start learning about the states of matter, they often apply macroscopic qualities to particles and describe them as hard, soft and able to melt. Some misconceptions that you might encounter are that children think that:

- a particle means a piece of the solid not a particle at the atomic level;

- particles have different shapes, eg round and usually small for a gas, cuboid and usually large for a solid;

- particles in a liquid are further apart than in a solid;

- a gas has no weight;

- when liquids evaporate they disappear forever;

- the water droplets seen on a cold container due to condensation are there because water that was inside the vessel has moved outside;

- boiling is an irreversible change: ie when water becomes steam it can never become water again;

- weight increases when a liquid changes to a solid and decreases when it changes back to a liquid;

- when salt or sugar is added to water it disappears and does not contribute to the mass of the solution;

- when something burns it no longer exists;

- rusting is ageing rather than a chemical change.

Be prepared for children confusing the processes of melting and dissolving and thinking the latter is a chemical change. This difference is discussed later (see page 79). Children find it difficult to understand the differences between reversible and irreversible changes of materials.

FACTFILE

A material is the matter from which substances are made. Materials can be solids, liquids or gases. Materials are sometimes classified into categories such as metal, plastic, ceramic, glass or fibre.

Reversible change is a change that can be undone. It may alter how a material looks or feels but new materials are not created. It can include a change in shape (mechanical change), change in state (heating and cooling), as seen in Figure 6.1, and mixing of substances (dissolving). At the atomic level, the atoms and molecules seen in Figure 6.1 as a unit consisting of one white circle with two black circles remain the same, but the configuration between the units changes due to the addition or reduction of energy. The processes involved in reversible change include melting, freezing, evaporating, condensing and dissolving. Reversible change is also known as physical change.

Irreversible change is a change where new materials are formed. These changes are permanent and cannot be undone. At the atomic level, bonds between atoms and molecules are broken and new bonds are made. Examples of irreversible changes include cooking, burning, firing clay and rusting. When you toast bread, you cannot get the bread back the way it was before it was toasted. The term chemical change is sometimes used to refer to irreversible changes but note that not all chemical changes are irreversible. In primary schools it is best to use the term irreversible change.

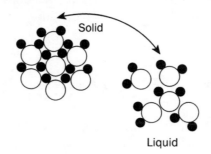

Figure 6.1 *Change of state from a solid to a liquid/liquid to solid (reversible)*

Topics and teaching strategies

Everyday materials and their uses

The new curriculum (DfE, 2013) suggests pupils in Year 1 should be taught to

- *distinguish between an object and the material from which it is made;*
- *identify and name a variety of everyday materials, including wood, plastic, glass, metal, water and rock.*

(DFE, 2013, page 149)

By Year 2 pupils should be taught to

identify and compare the uses of a variety of everyday materials including wood, metal, plastic, glass, brick, rock, paper and cardboard.

(DfE, 2013, page 153)

An effective way of starting this topic would be to do an elicitation activity where you ask the children *What is a material?* This can then be followed by another question which asks them to provide you with some examples of different types of materials. Keep reinforcing the fact that all objects are made up of different materials to overcome the possible misconception that the term material only refers to fabrics. Using the story of the *Three Little Pigs* and the fact that their houses are made of different materials can reinforce the point and provides a useful literary link for young children.

You could encourage your pupils to investigate different objects and the materials they are made of by walking round the school and naming the objects and what they are made of, eg door made of wood, window made of glass, tiles made of ceramic. Be prepared for young children to find this difficult to do, as they often struggle with making a distinction between the object and what it is made of. The next stage might be to show how an object can be made of different materials such as a spoon which can be made of plastic, wood or metal. A specific material can also be used for a number of different objects, so metal can be used for cans, kettles, nails or jewellery. It is important for children to explore a range of materials to include brick, paper, fabric, elastic and foil. A trip with a historic focus, eg to a watermill, can consolidate knowledge of why certain materials were used in the past for certain functions. Young children might work scientifically and perform simple tests to explore *Which is the best material for a raincoat for teddy to keep him dry?* Older children might compare the uses of everyday materials at home and school. This would encourage the development of scientific skills such as observation, and children might record these observations by using tables (*working scientifically*).

By the time children are in Year 5 they should be taught to

> give reasons, based on evidence from comparative and fair tests, for the particular use of everyday materials, including metals, wood and plastic.
>
> (DfE, 2013, page 169)

FACTFILE

A fair test is a test which is carried out where one factor is changed and the effect of that factor on another factor is measured, while keeping other factors the same. The term 'variable' is sometimes used instead of factor.

You might involve children to devise a fair test to see which material might be best to block out noise or keep a mug of tea warm (*working scientifically*). These types of investigations, considering the uses of different materials, help pupils to develop an understanding of conductors and insulators. Once children can identify different materials and think of their uses, they are ready to consider the physical properties of materials and group them accordingly.

Grouping of materials according to physical properties

Pupils should be taught to

> compare and group together a variety of everyday materials on the basis of their simple physical properties.
>
> (DfE, 2013, page 149)

Hands-on displays of objects are very effective in encouraging young children to explore different types of materials. You could also provide older children with a list of vocabulary to help them describe the materials, including words such as shiny, bendy, rough, smooth, hard and soft. The *Guess What I Am*, game where one child describes their material to others who cannot see it using this vocabulary is something you could try, or the tried and tested feely box where children put their hands in a box and guess what is inside.

The next stage might be to give children a list of objects made of different materials and ask them to sort them out into those that are hard/soft, rough/smooth, bendy/not bendy. This can be extended by using other categories such as those that float/sink and those that are magnetic/non-magnetic. You might decide not to prompt the children by providing the categories, but just ask them to sort them into distinct groups. You will generally find that young children will sort objects and the materials they are made of by observable features such as rough/smooth, whereas older children will sort them by function. Using large hoops and asking the children to place their items inside using Venn diagrams (Figure 6.2) is an excellent visual way of sorting items and a useful link with work you may be covering in mathematics. It is also a great way of making the point that sometimes objects are made up of more than one material, in which case some of the hoops need to overlap.

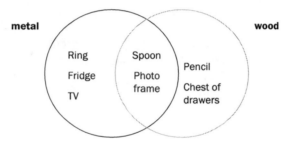

Figure 6.2 Sorting objects made of different materials using Venn diagrams

Older children or more able children could be introduced to terms such as durability, hardness, viscosity, strength and ductility. Having a ball with these words written on and playing a game where you throw the ball to a child who has to try and explain one of the terms before throwing the ball to another, not only helps to develop understanding, but is also an excellent way of focusing attention in an introduction or plenary to a lesson.

As children get older, they should be encouraged to think about the properties of materials and their suitability (or otherwise) for particular purposes. You could ask them to come up with unusual and creative uses for everyday materials.

There are lots of opportunities to allow children to work scientifically. Children could investigate how well toy cars move on different surfaces, eg carpet, lino, wood and tiles in order to devise and carry out a fair test. Older children might investigate the durability of a range of fabrics using a stone for rubbing to carry out the investigation. More able children might investigate the absorbency of paper towels based on their physical properties and change a variable, such as the amount of liquid poured, or the type of liquid.

Mechanical change

The national curriculum states that in Year 1 pupils should be taught to

> *find out how the shapes of solid objects made from some materials can be changed by squashing, bending, twisting and stretching.*
>
> (DfE, 2013, page 153)

FACTFILE

Mechanical change refers to changing the appearance of an object by applying a force such as squashing, bending, twisting or stretching. The resultant change will reflect the properties of that material. With some materials, the mechanical change will be reversible if the material is deformed within its elastic limit.

Children can experiment changing the appearance of materials such as modelling clay, but you should also provide them with opportunities of using other materials such as sponges, springs and hard materials such as metals or wood. You could set them the challenge of trying to make a boat float using modelling clay, and link it with work on forces. Ask pupils to describe the action they are using to change their material and whether they can change the material back to the way it was before, by applying another type of action. You could link this activity to work in food technology where children are rolling out dough or pastry.

States of matter

The national curriculum states that by the time children are in Year 4 they should know about the states of matter and should be taught to:

- *compare and group materials together, according to whether they are solids, liquids or gases;*
- *observe that some materials change state when they are heated or cooled, and measure or research the temperature at which this happens in degrees Celsius (°C);*
- *identify the part played by evaporation and condensation in the water cycle and associate the rate of evaporation with temperature.*

> (DfE, 2013, page 162)

FACTFILE

Scientists believe that all matter is made up of particles (particulate theory) which are very small and may be atoms of an element or molecules of a compound.

An **atom** is the simplest type of particle. All matter (material) is made up of atoms such as oxygen or hydrogen.

Molecules form when atoms bond together. Molecules therefore consist of a number of atoms bonded together that can vary from two to many thousands. Water, for example, is a molecule made up of two atoms of hydrogen and one of oxygen (H_2O).

An **element** is a substance made up of only one kind of atom. There are over 100 elements that have been identified, such as helium.

A **compound** is a substance made of different types of atoms of different elements; for example, water is made of atoms of the element hydrogen and atoms of the element oxygen.

Particles are believed to be in constant motion (kinetic theory). In a solid the particles are closely packed and arranged in a regular pattern. They vibrate about a fixed point and there is no other movement. There is a strong bond between neighbouring particles, as seen in Figure 6.3.

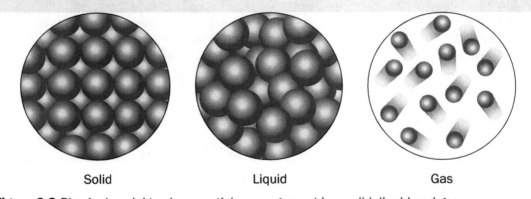

| Solid | Liquid | Gas |

Figure 6.3 *Physical model to show particle arrangement in a solid, liquid and gas*

In a liquid the particles are fairly closely packed but not arranged in a regular pattern. They do not move apart as it is often thought, but they are not fixed in a position either. They are thus free to slide over one another and they are weakly bonded to neighbouring particles. A useful analogy is to liken the particles in a liquid to the movement of balls in a soft-play indoor area where the balls do not move apart from each other, but slide over one another.

In a gas, the particles are widely spread out and not arranged in a regular pattern. They are free to move in all directions and are not bonded to neighbouring particles. This is an opportunity to reinforce the point that the particles in all three states of matter are the same: ie in Figure 6.3 they are all red balls.

An interesting elicitation exercise might be to ask children to draw and name different types of solids, liquids and gases to see what their initial understanding of these scientific terms is.

Then you can explore characteristics of solids, liquids and gases by giving examples of each and asking children to come up with a list of characteristics that they have in common. Be prepared to guide them through the exercise with the use of questions. Hopefully they will recognise that solids are not easily compressed, they are a fixed shape and volume and can be heavy or light. With liquids they may say that they are not easily compressed, they do not have a fixed shape or volume and can be heavy or light. Equally with gases, prompt them to realise that they can be easily compressed, they are of no fixed shape, have a variable volume and are very light in comparison to solids and liquids. This may be a good opportunity to mention that a gas is also a material and that not all gases are poisonous.

A natural progression from the above might be to do a sorting activity. Your list of items might include jelly, milk, polystyrene, cotton wool, water, air, chocolate, treacle and talcum powder. Ask pupils to sort them into solids, liquids and gases using the Venn diagrams described previously. Provide an interesting variety of items which will challenge any misconceptions they might have, such as all solids are hard and heavy, or all liquids flow easily. The latter will depend on the viscosity of the liquid. Including items such as powders will challenge them further, as many children think that powders are not solids. Be careful not to include items such as toothpaste or hair mousse which cannot be classified as solids, liquids or gases but are in fact colloids.

FACTFILE

A colloid is a type of chemical mixture where one substance is dispersed evenly throughout another. All colloids thus consist of two substances which cannot mix properly or fully with each other. The particles of the dispersed substance are only suspended in the mixture, unlike a solution where they are completely dissolved within. Cornflour mixed in water is often used in Early Years and Key Stage 1 because it has an interesting texture and behaves like a solid but also as a liquid; it is in fact a colloid. Muddy water is another example of a colloid.

By upper Key Stage 2 children will be expected to have a broader understanding of materials and be able to group everyday materials using additional properties as well as those covered in previous years. In Year 5, for example, pupils should be taught to

> compare and group together everyday materials on the basis of their properties including their hardness, solubility, transparency, conductivity (electrical and thermal) and response to magnets.

> (DfE, 2013, page 169)

This could entail children comparing materials and deciding which material would be the best to make a switch for their circuit.

Children will now be ready to explore changes of state which are reversible and particulate theory can be used to explain how solids, liquids and gases are interchangeable as a result of an increase or decrease in heat energy. Thus, when an object is heated, the motion of the particles increases as the particles become more energetic. If it is cooled the motion of the particles decreases as they lose energy. Physical models are a useful way of introducing the concept of particle arrangement but stress that when a solid melts, the particles do become excited and break free of their physical bonds, but do not move further apart. Children could model the above through role play and drama and pretend to be particles of solids, then liquids, then gases and vary their motion as they gain energy. They could explore the effects of temperature on different substances such as chocolate and butter and measure the temperature in degrees Celsius using a thermometer, after being shown how to use one. Using chocolate and butter is important as many young children often think that only ice melts. Children can undergo some research into the temperature at which certain materials change from a solid to a liquid to a gas or vice versa. They might *work scientifically* by investigating the temperature at which different materials melt or evaporate.

FACTFILE

Be aware that water is a poor example to show expansion when melting. In ice, the solid particles take up more space than corresponding liquid particles: ie the particles in the ice are further apart than in water, so water expands when it freezes.

Freezing is used to describe a liquid turning into a solid when its temperature is lowered below its freezing point.

If children have discussed the water cycle in geography, they can identify the parts played by evaporation and condensation in this cycle. Children have some interesting ideas about what happens to water in a puddle. Try an elicitation activity where you ask them to complete a sequenced diagram like the one shown in Figure 6.4 where a child is explaining what will happen to water in the puddle in the playground during various times in the day. Prompt them to explain where the water has gone and explain that it has not disappeared.

Morning	Break time	Lunchtime	Home time

Figure 6.4 *Sequenced diagram to show what happens to water in a puddle during the day once it has stopped raining*

Alternatively, ask the children to draw round a puddle in the playground using chalk during different times of the day, so they will be able to see how the puddle starts to shrink. Refer to everyday experiences such as hanging out washing on a line to dry and develop scientific skills by asking them to investigate how different temperatures might affect the drying of the clothes. Place petri dishes with water in different locations around the school and predict which might evaporate more quickly and why. One way of demonstrating how condensation occurs is to model this with a boiling kettle and a cool plate held carefully above the steam. Children can then observe the water droplets that will form on the plate and try to explain why this has occurred. Prompt them to think where the water on the plate is coming from.

FACTFILE

The water cycle depicted in Figure 6.5 describes the continuous movement of water on, above and below the surface of the Earth. It has no fixed starting point, but you can start explaining what happens with the oceans: the Sun heats the water and some of it evaporates and changes from a liquid to a gaseous state known as water vapour. Air currents take the water vapour up into the atmosphere where the cooler temperature causes it to condense into clouds. Eventually the particles that make up the water vapour collide and grow and fall out of the sky as precipitation, which is rain or snow. Most of this precipitation falls back to the oceans and land as runoff. Some of this runoff will enter rivers in valleys and oceans where the whole process begins again.

Evaporation

Within a liquid some particles will have more energy than others and may have sufficient energy to escape from the surface of the liquid as gas or vapour. Evaporation takes place at room temperature which is often well below the boiling point of the liquid. As the temperature increases, the rate of evaporation will increase until the air becomes saturated. Windy conditions assist evaporation by helping to move the vapour particles from the surface of the liquid so that more can escape to the surface.

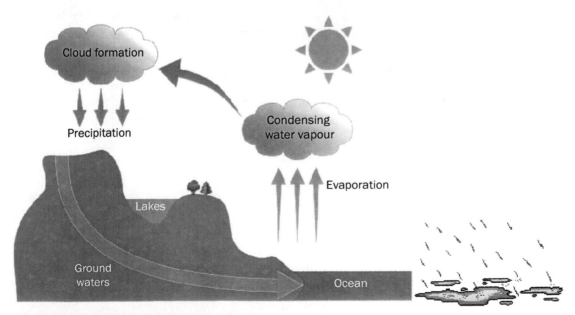

Figure 6.5 The water cycle

Reversible change

Pupils in Year 5 should:

- *know that some materials will dissolve in liquid to form a solution, and describe how to recover a substance from a solution;*

- *use knowledge of solids, liquids and gases to decide how mixtures might be separated, including through filtering, sieving and evaporating;*

- *demonstrate that dissolving, mixing and changes of state are reversible changes.*

(DfE, 2013, page 169)

FACTFILE

Some substances dissolve when they are mixed with water. When a substance dissolves it might look like it has disappeared, but it is in fact mixed with the water to make a liquid called a solution, eg salt dissolved in water. The solute is the salt, and the liquid, in this case the water, is the solvent. Substances that dissolve in water are called soluble. Those that do not dissolve in water are called insoluble. Heat and stirring can help substances dissolve faster in water. Dissolving is a physical change and is reversible. The salty water can be changed back into water and salt through the process of evaporation.

A mixture is the name given to two or more substances including elements which are added together without a chemical change taking place. Muddy water is an example of a mixture.

Children can investigate to see which materials will dissolve in water and which ones will not. Use the digital microscope to help them predict which materials will dissolve better based on the size of the particles (*working scientifically*). Provide them with a range of items such as sugar, salt, flour, coffee and rice. More able children can be allowed to test whether the temperature of the water will affect how well a material dissolves. This exercise might allow them to draw and interpret line graphs when recording their results. Alternatively, ask them to test whether a solute dissolves quicker in different solvents. They should also consider whether the material added has contributed to the mass of the solution. At this stage be prepared to deal with misconceptions regarding melting and dissolving as children often confuse the two.

FACTFILE

Dissolving can happen without heating. It requires two or more substances and usually involves a solid being added to a liquid. Dissolving cannot be reversed by cooling and can be described as two different kinds of particles intimately mixed together.

Melting only needs one substance and heat is needed for it to occur. The substance remains pure after melting and involves a solid changing into a liquid. Melting can be reversed by cooling and involves the rearrangement of particles.

An exciting activity for the children is to make a mixture made up of different materials. Pose them a problem and say that you have mixed this list of items with water (sand, salt, pebbles, nails, pasta shells) and ask them to consider different ways of separating the mixture to get back the original items. The materials made up of the heavier particles can be separated using a sieve. Those with finer particles can be separated by using filters. The nails can be separated by using magnets and the salt can be retrieved by evaporating the water that has been left after all the other materials have been taken out. Allow the children to come up with the suggestions. An alternative activity is to give them some water with soil, mud and stones in it and ask pupils to make the muddy water clean. They could experiment and use different types of filters to separate the different items, but in fact if they left this solution in a lemonade bottle, for example, over a period of time, the various components would settle into layers according to the size of their particles. (See Chapter 8 on Rocks and soils, page 99.)

FACTFILE

Chromatography is the term used to describe the separation of constituents, for example different inks travelling at different speeds within a mixture, which causes the different inks to separate.

Drop some good quality black ink on some filter paper and then, using a water dropper, put some drops of water onto the filter paper. You will see the black ink split up into its component inks which will include colours such as yellow and blue. Chromatography is another example of a reversible change.

Irreversible change

By the end of Year 5 pupils should be able to

> explain that some changes result in the formation of new materials, and that this kind of change is not usually reversible, including changes associated with burning and the action of acid on bicarbonate of soda.

> (DfE, 2013, page 169)

There are many exciting activities that can be done with children to help them understand that sometimes changes lead to the formation of new materials and this kind of change is often irreversible. Baking a cake is a good example to refer to because once the flour, butter and sugar have been mixed and the mixture placed in the oven to be baked, the original ingredients cannot be retrieved and a new product has been made. Doing an investigation where children explore nails rusting is another way of showing a chemical change which is difficult to reverse.

FACTFILE

Rusting is a chemical change where both water and oxygen are required for iron to rust. Rusting takes place in two stages: firstly, the atoms of iron react with the atoms of oxygen in the air to form iron oxide. Then the molecules of iron oxide combine with molecules of water to form molecules of hydrated iron oxide. Rust is therefore the common name for hydrated iron oxide.

Ask the children to set up clear containers and place a nail in each. Fill one container with water, leave another one with just air, and the third with water but place some oil over the top, and leave them for about a week. Ask the children to predict what they think will happen first. The nail in the water will rust because there is water and dissolved air. The nail in the air will rust too because there is water in the air, but the nail with the water and layer of oil will not rust because the oil prevents air getting into the water.

Another way of illustrating a change which cannot be reversed is by making pop rockets. Place half an Alka-Seltzer tablet on the inside lid of a film canister and fasten the tablet to the lid with a piece of Blu-Tack. Pour water into the canister until it is one-third full, fasten the lid tightly and place upside down on a table on top of a paper towel. Stand well clear of the table and wait. After a few moments, the Alka-Seltzer tablet will react with the water and produce carbon dioxide, which will cause the lid to explode open and the rocket will fly upwards and might even hit the ceiling. As with fireworks, do not return immediately to the film canister. If you are patient and you have measured all the items correctly it will work.

CROSS-CURRICULAR LINKS

Materials and their properties is a topic which not only lends itself to lots of practical work, but can also be linked to other areas of the curriculum.

Literacy

Children could research the work of Ruth Benerito, who invented wrinkle-free cotton, and write a newspaper article. They might write a story in the first person based on the water cycle, for example a day in the life of a water droplet or undertake some instructional writing about how to make a pop rocket.

Research, using the internet or books, into inventors of materials such as John Dunlop, is a useful exercise in developing literary skills.

Numeracy

In mathematics children might sort different materials according to their properties and use Venn diagrams, or use tables to record how long it takes a material to dissolve. They might use line graphs, if they have used temperature sensors while investigating the insulating properties of different materials when trying to keep tea warm.

Other curricular areas

In history children might research the different materials used by the Egyptians such as papyrus, or those used by the Victorians as part of their daily lives. In music they might create a rap to explain the water cycle. In computing they might use the internet to carry out some research into who invented plastic. In design and technology they might consider the different properties of materials that would be suitable to make a vehicle.

HEALTH AND SAFETY

Be Safe in Science (ASE, 2010) provides some useful information on things to take into consideration when teaching this topic and is a good source of reference, along with the following:

- make sure that the materials you use are safe for the children to handle;

- take care if heating/burning any items and take advice on which materials should not be heated or burnt in an enclosed area such as a primary classroom;

- if demonstrating the process of condensation using steam from a kettle, ensure that you carry out the demonstration yourself.

Critical questions

On a scale of 1–10 (with 10 being completely confident) how confident do you now feel in your own subject knowledge of materials and their properties as a topic?

» *Identify the specific areas where you feel less confident.*

» *Where else might you look and what else might you do to develop your subject knowledge in those areas?*

» *What resources do you need to collect in order to successfully start teaching this topic?*

» *Where might you take pupils in order to develop their subject knowledge? Are there any school visits you could do?*

Taking it further

Russell, T and Watt, D (1990) *Materials, SPACE Research Report*. Liverpool: Liverpool University Press.

Websites

www.bbc.bitesize.co.uk

www.chem4kids.com

www.stevespanglerscience.com/tp://marshallbrain.com/science

www.teachersmedia.co.uk/videos/materials-activities

References

ASE (2010) *Be Safe in Science*. Hatfield: ASE.

DfE (2013) *Teachers' Standards*. www.gov.uk/government/uploads/system/uploads/attachment_data/file/208682/Teachers__Standards_2013.pdf (accessed 17 February 2014).

7   Earth and space

Introduction

Earth and space is an area of science which fascinates many children, but it is full of abstract and difficult concepts that make it difficult to understand. When you teach this topic you will be asking children to go beyond their concrete experiences and model situations which at times they may find counter-intuitive.

The Earth and space is relevant to children from a very early age as they become aware of the stars, the occurrence of day and night and seasonal changes. As children get older the focus for your teaching will extend to exploring and understanding how our knowledge of space has evolved, as well as developing an understanding of the Moon, the planets, the Solar System and celestial movements. When you teach this topic it is important that you establish links to other related science topics such as light, forces and energy. Although it is important not to underestimate children's abilities and levels of understanding in this area, it is useful to promote their conceptual development through the use of models, role play, practical hands-on activities and the use of secondary resources.

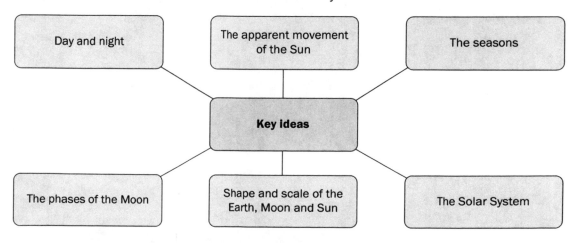

KEY VOCABULARY

The new national curriculum (DfE, 2013) stresses the importance of children using technical terminology accurately and precisely and building up an extended specialist vocabulary.

In Key Stage 1 children should begin to learn and to explore the basic vocabulary to describe objects that can be easily observed in the sky. This will involve children becoming familiar with vocabulary such as **Earth**, **Sun** and **Moon**. Other vocabulary such as **space**, **planets** and **stars** can be introduced later. During Year 1 you will start helping children explore seasonal changes. This will entail pupils becoming familiar with and learning vocabulary linked to the seasons, ie **autumn**, **winter**, **spring** and **summer**, and **day length**, ie **dawn**, **daybreak**, **midday**, **dusk**, **evening** and **night**.

It is in upper Key Stage 2, Year 5 that you will continue to develop pupils' vocabulary linked to the Earth and space. Pupils should be using key vocabulary such as **Solar System**, the eight planets: **Mercury**, **Venus**, **Earth**, **Mars**, **Jupiter**, **Saturn**, **Uranus** and **Neptune** (Pluto was reclassified as a 'dwarf planet' in 2006) and understand that the Moon is a celestial body. Key words linked to planetary motion should include **rotate**, **revolve**, **orbit**, **spin**, **axis**, **gravity** and **hemispheres**. The study of the Moon will involve pupils learning terminology such as the **summer solstice**, **winter solstice**, **spring equinox**, **autumn equinox**, **gibbous moon**, **crescent moon** and **waxing** and **waning**. Since pupils will be considering astronomical clocks the words **sundial** and **gnomon** will also need to be introduced.

CHILDREN'S IDEAS AND COMMON MISCONCEPTIONS

During the study of this topic children will hold various misconceptions about the Earth, Moon, Sun, planets and celestial motion. At an early age these may consist of the following:

- the Earth is flat and stationary;

- the Moon and the Sun remain stationary;

- day and night are caused by the Sun going behind a hill, clouds covering the Sun or even the Moon covering the Sun;

- the Sun and the Moon have been made by human or divine agents.

Further misconceptions that may become apparent as children learn more about the topic are that:

- the Solar System rotates round the Earth and that the Earth lies at the centre of the Solar System with the Sun and planets orbiting it;

- the Earth is larger than the Sun and the Moon which are larger than the stars;
- the Sun moves across the sky and that causes day and night;
- the Sun goes round the Earth once a day;
- the Earth goes round the Sun once a day;
- the seasons are caused because the Earth is closer to the Sun in the summer;
- the Sun is not a star;
- the Moon and planets are primary sources of light;
- a star and a planet are the same thing;
- gravity exists as an absolute down force which is at right angles to the plane of the Earth and sky and there is no gravity on the Moon.

It is important that before you start teaching this topic you find out pupils' prior understanding as it will help you focus your teaching and give you information about any misconceptions held. In Key Stage 1 this can be done by asking probing questions while in Key Stage 2 this may be achieved by the use of a quiz.

Elicitation

An elicitation activity such as the one below can be an effective exercise for you to carry out with top Key Stage 2 children to assess their knowledge and understanding of the topic. You can ask them to complete the quiz relying on their first instinctive answer. After you have completed the topic it will be useful to ask the children to return to their original answers and review them so that they too can establish how their misconceptions have been addressed.

Earth and space quiz

Write true or false after each statement.

1. We can see the Moon because it reflects light from the Sun. (True)
2. We can see planets because they give out their own light. (False)
3. It is cold in winter because the Sun is further away. (False)
4. The Sun is a star. (True)
5. The planets are nearer to Earth than the stars. (True)
6. The Moon appears to change its shape because the Earth casts different shadows onto its surface. (False)
7. The Sun appears to be higher in the sky during the summer. (True)

8.   The Sun orbits the Earth once every 24 hours. (False)

9.   The Moon orbits the Earth once every day. (False)

10. From the Earth we always see the same side of the Moon. (True)

11. There is no gravity on the Moon. (False)

12. It is safe to observe a solar eclipse through sunglasses. (False)

13. The Moon is the major cause of ocean tides. (True)

14. The Moon is always visible at night. (False)

15. It is hotter at the Equator because it is nearer the Sun. (False)

16. The stars are only there at night. (False)

17. Everywhere in England gets dark at the same time. (False)

18. The Earth moves round the Sun once each day. (False)

19. The Moon phases depend on the portion of the illuminated Moon which we can see on Earth. (True)

20. Orbiting satellites stay up in orbit because the outward force balances the inward pull of gravity. (True)

21. Winter happens because there are more clouds to block out the Sun. (False)

22. The seasons happen because of the weather and plants. (False)

Topics and teaching strategies

The shape and scale of the Earth, Moon and Sun

As the new curriculum suggests children need to

> *describe the Sun, Earth and Moon as approximately spherical bodies.*
> (DfE, 2013, page 170)

The majority of children you will teach in Key Stage 2 will be aware that the Sun, Earth and Moon are approximately spherical. There will nonetheless be those children who do not wholly believe this to be true. Ask your pupils to draw what they think the Earth would look like if viewed from outer space and then ask them to explain their drawings to each other. Always make sure that the children understand the difference between a circle and a sphere. You may be surprised by what you hear.

You could ask children to then carry out some research into the historical development of scientific ideas about the Earth and its shape and even visit the Flat Earth Society website which still exists today! You can further reinforce the idea that the Sun, Earth and Moon are approximately spherical by using the Earth and Moon Viewer (see Taking it further at the end of this chapter) which views the Earth from the Sun, the Moon, the night side of the Earth, above any location on the planet specified by latitude, longitude and altitude, from a satellite in the Earth's orbit, or above various cities around the globe. In addition to the Earth, you can also view the Moon from the Earth, Sun, night side, named formations on the lunar surface or as a map showing day and night. Alternatively, the NASA website provides you with an excellent photograph of the Earth taken from Apollo 8 in 1968. You can get children to use secondary sources of information in order to aid understanding, ie *working scientifically*. They could also be asked to point out where they live on a 3D globe of the Earth.

You will find that children do not think that the Sun is a star and do not understand the difference between a star and a planet. These concepts will need explaining to them.

FACTFILE

Our Sun is our nearest star at a distance of 150,000,000km away from Earth. It is 100 times the diameter of the Earth and composed of hot gases, mainly hydrogen and helium. It is the only object in the Solar System that produces its own heat and is at the centre of the Solar System. It contains 99.8% of the mass of the Solar System so there is a great gravitational force between the Sun and the rest of the Solar System, strong enough to hold the planets in place.

A useful activity to help children have a better understanding of the Sun is to draw a picture of the Sun and then get them to compare their picture to one taken by a telescope, eg Hubble. This will enable children to understand that the Sun does not have points, radiating rays and that the Sun is not in fact solid and evenly hot but it is in fact a seething mass of gas.

Gravity

Many children also have difficulty in understanding the concept of 'down' in relation to gravity. You could assess their understanding of how objects fall on Earth by asking them to show an object falling to the ground at differing places on a diagram of the Earth, eg North Pole, South Pole, Equator. This is a difficult task to do as it requires children to have some understanding of gravity and how the force of gravity causes objects to fall towards the centre of the Earth. However, you may find they will show an object falling perpendicular to where they are stood and not towards the centre of the Earth. In order to explain their drawings and their understanding of gravity you will need to discuss this misconception with them.

Day and night

When studying Earth and space children need to

> use the idea of the Earth's rotation to explain day and night and the apparent movement of the Sun across the sky.

> (DfE, 2013, page 170)

Time

Before children can fully understand the idea of the Earth's rotation, it is important for you to reinforce the notion of time passing, estimating its passing and also know about how it can be measured. In order to develop this idea, an interesting activity is first of all to get pupils to estimate how long a minute is or how long it would take them to do a particular task, and then ask them how long they think a day, a month or a year are. Many Key Stage 1 children will confuse how long a day is (24 hours) with daylight hours and would give a response such as 12 hours, though this is less likely with Key Stage 2 children. You will constantly need to reinforce that 24 hours makes a day and perhaps model it with a globe and talk about the units of time. You can ask children to think about the daily events in a day and perhaps sequence the activities that they do in a day. Though the length of a month will be harder for pupils to remember and to understand given that it can vary between 28 and 31 days, the rhyme *Thirty Days Has September, April June and November* may prove a useful mnemonic for pupils.

To further their understanding of how the Earth moves around the Sun anti-clockwise in a year and that it takes 365.25 days to do this, use a globe and torch for the Sun to model this idea. Remember to explain to children that the four quarters over four years are added together to make a leap year. You could ask children to demonstrate their understanding of the passage of time in a year by drawing a timeline of major events, for example Christmas and their birthdays.

The movement of the Earth

Many children think that the Sun simply rises upwards in the morning then sets downwards at night. They do not take into account that the Sun is seen to move across the sky. It is important with this part of Earth and space to use as many kinaesthetic experiences as possible to model learning and help pupils to understand these difficult concepts. You could use a south-facing window and stand on the same spot in the room and use sticky circles to plot the apparent movement across the sky every hour. Do this once a week over a four-week period. You could ask the children to present their findings in oral or written form and provide an explanation (*working scientifically*). You will find this a useful assessment task.

You could also ask the children to try out the following activity to help them develop their understanding of day and night. Ask the children to work in groups of four to act out the movements of how the Earth spins on its axis in a day and its position in relation to the Sun. Remember to stress to children that it takes the Earth 24 hours to spin on its axis. One child can represent the Earth, another the Sun and the other two children can explain what is happening. The children can be substituted for a torch or preferably an overhead projector representing the Sun and a real globe. You could place a plasticine figure on the UK on the globe and this representation will show the children how night occurs on the Earth as it spins anti-clockwise, with one half of the Earth being illuminated by the Sun and the other half being left in darkness.

You can further reinforce all of these concepts by using the Earth and Moon Viewer (see Taking it further), where you can view a map of the Earth showing the day and night regions at this moment. This aspect of children's study can now be linked to time zones around the world and may be reinforced during numeracy. By encouraging children to investigate time zones on the internet you can encourage children to use secondary sources of information (*working scientifically*) to further develop this idea.

By getting children to draw round shadows in the playground you can provide an exciting activity to see how shadows change over the course of a day and their directions. Asking children questions about what made the shadow and why they move during the day can help to assess children's understanding of such concepts; for example, do they understand where the Sun rises and sets? An important point to note relates to the statement that the Sun is directly overhead at midday. Please remember this is only true during the summer solstice and if you are in an equatorial region.

You can further develop the concept of the change in shadows over time and the patterns associated with shadows by developing the following enquiry: place a stick on the school playground on a sunny day and then mark the position and length of the shadow using chalk. As the day goes by the children should note the changes in the lengths of the shadows which can be recorded on a spreadsheet and then shown graphically (*working scientifically*). This work can also be linked to recordings of a sundial gnomon which is angled rather than vertical. You can explore with the children how the gnomon's angle should equal the latitude where this activity is taking place. You could also carry out these activities at different times in the year noting the change in shadow length and angle. This can be linked to further work on seasonal changes since in summer the Sun's pathway in the sky is higher so there will be shorter shadows formed, while in the winter the Sun has a lower pathway therefore longer shadows will be formed.

You can encourage children to take photos, using a digital camera, of the shadows they have observed at different times of the year. These then can be used to explain the difference between a summer and winter shadow (*working scientifically*).

The year and seasons

Children need to:

- *observe changes across the four seasons;*
- *observe and describe weather associated with the seasons and how day length varies.*

(DfE, 2013, page 150)

As statutory guidance suggests, children at Key Stage 1 or at Key Stage 2 are not required to know what causes seasonal changes but you will find it difficult to talk to the children about the seasons, especially at Key Stage 2, without referring to what causes them as children often have the misconception that the seasons are caused by the Earth's distance from the Sun and not the tilt of the Earth, especially as the orbit of the Earth is nearly but not quite circular.

FACTFILE

When the Earth is furthest away from the Sun, the Northern Hemisphere is tilted towards the sun and experiencing summer. When the Earth is closest to the Sun, the Northern Hemisphere is experiencing winter. Distance will make a difference to the amount of heat energy received from the Sun but it is the tilt of the Earth which is the significant factor.

An initial activity you could do with the children in Key Stage 1 to help them relate the seasons to their own experiences is to ask the children to draw a picture of the same scene during different seasons, for example their garden or a park. You will also find this a valuable record of assessment. You can assess their understanding by asking them questions about what happens to the trees, plants and animals at different times of the year. You can take children outside so they can collect items (preferably those on the ground) which will illustrate the different colours of nature throughout the four seasons and then stick leaves or petals on a card. You can also turn this into a sorting activity by having a list of statements or pictures of what happens to differing objects during the different seasons. You can ask them to sort them first of all into summer and winter and then extend this further by considering autumn and spring. You can continue to relate the seasons to children's own experiences by asking them to recall what they do in the different seasons, what they eat and what they wear, holidays and leisure. These observations can then be recorded into a class log book in the form of pictures or writing.

In Key Stage 2 children can record the variation in day length daily which perhaps can be recorded in the form of a table (*working scientifically*), in order to help them understand that there are longer days in summer.

You need to encourage children to be aware of the weather and to discuss and record the weather using pictures or charts. You might encourage children to record aspects of the weather such as rainfall and use ICT to display it graphically. They will thus be gathering and recording data (*working scientifically*). You could ask children to discuss the weather in different parts of the world at that particular time or when they go on holiday.

When discussing the seasons and helping pupils to start building a mental model of what causes them, a useful visual activity for you to extend more able Year 6 children might be to ask them to act out how the Earth moves around the Sun in a year. One child can stand in the centre of a space with a strong torch representing the Sun and the other can orbit the Sun anti-clockwise calling out the different seasons in the Northern Hemisphere.

A more advanced alternative is to ask the child who is representing the Earth to hold a globe of the Earth keeping the tilt the same as the Earth's axis at 23.5 degrees to the vertical. When the globe is in position (a) (see Figure 7.1) in the winter solstice position, the Northern Hemisphere is tilting away from the Sun so it is winter in the Northern Hemisphere and summer in the Southern Hemisphere. They can also observe how the North Pole is in perpetual darkness and the South Pole in perpetual light even when the globe is spun to represent a day. It is important that you get children to model a day so children can see that this is the case throughout the 24 hours of the day. Also you can point out how the hours of daylight will increase as you move from the North Pole down to the Equator and then further down

Summer and winter

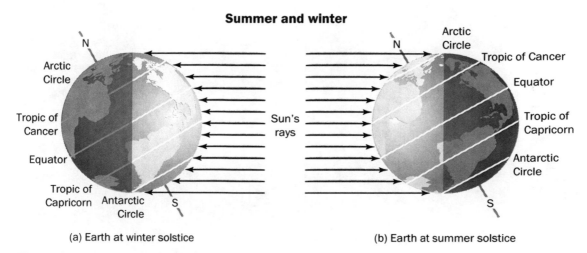

(a) Earth at winter solstice   (b) Earth at summer solstice

Figure 7.1 *The Earth at summer and winter solstice*

to the South Pole. Use names of cities and their hours of daylight to reinforce this. When the globe is moved to the spring equinox position, the angle of the axis remains the same (23.5 degrees to the vertical) and the Northern Hemisphere is halfway being tilted towards and away from the Sun. It makes no difference to the daylight hours as the line which divides the half of the globe which is lit from the half of the globe which is dark will pass through both poles. Once you reach the summer solstice position (b) (see Figure 7.1), the Northern Hemisphere is tilting towards the Sun and the Southern Hemisphere is tilting away from the Sun. Draw their attention to the fact that the North Pole is now in perpetual light and the South Pole is in perpetual darkness even when you spin the globe to represent a day. Then move the globe to the autumn equinox position keeping the tilt the same. The Northern Hemisphere is again halfway between being tilted away from and towards the Sun. The angle of the axis, as in the spring equinox, makes no difference to the amount of hours of daylight. You can also use web-based simulations to reinforce these concepts.

Children might still not understand why it is hotter in the summer and the link to the position of the Sun in the sky. Figure 7.2 may help you explain this. You can reinforce this idea with children by getting them to shine a strong torch at different angles and noting the area which is being lit up. They can draw an outline of the lit areas by using some chalk and then compare their different sizes. In the winter in the Northern Hemisphere the Sun can be seen lower down in the sky and covers a larger area and does not provide as much heat. In the summer the Sun would be higher in the sky in the Northern Hemisphere and the Sun's rays would fall on the Earth nearly vertically. It is important for you to mention at this stage that seasonal changes are not only due to the position of the Sun's rays on the Earth and that other factors such as proximity to the ocean also have an effect on the temperature.

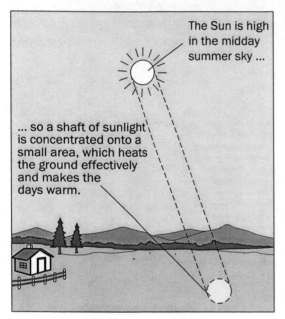
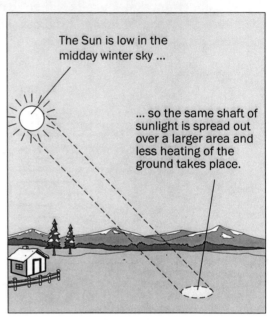

(a) The Sun in summer   (b) The Sun in winter

Figure 7.2 *The position of the Sun in the sky in summer and winter*

The Moon

Children need to

describe the movement of the Moon relative to the Earth.

(DfE, 2013, page 170)

FACTFILE

Our Moon is the Earth's only natural satellite and orbits the Earth once every 27 days and 7 hours. A moon is a celestial body that orbits a planet. We see our Moon because it is lit up by the Sun and is thus a secondary source of light. The Moon is about 0.25 the size of Earth and has one sixth of its gravity. The Moon is the major cause of the Earth's tides. As the Moon orbits the earth it draws or pulls the oceans towards it.

You can ask the children to find out how many moons other planets in the Solar System have, eg Jupiter.

The orbit of the Moon

You can ask the children to model the movement of the Moon around the Earth and the Earth around the Sun by getting them to work in groups of three in the playground in order to practise modelling this movement. Computer simulations can also be used to illustrate these relative movements. The Earth, Sun and Moon appear to be of similar size but are not due to the distances involved, eg the Sun appears smaller than it is because it is 150,000,000km away. This can be modelled by using objects of different sizes such as a basketball, a pepper-corn and a grain of sand.

FACTFILE

The Moon rotates on its axis at the same time as it orbits the Earth and in the same direction, anti-clockwise, thus we always see the same face of the Moon on Earth. When you see a full Moon everyone on the same side of the Earth will also see a full Moon. This also applies to all phases of the Moon.

To help children to understand this concept you can get them to attach a polystyrene ball to a stick and draw a black circle on the ball. Ask a child to sit on a chair in an empty space and they will represent Earth. Start turning the polystyrene ball round on the stick at the same time as you circle the chair with the child sitting on. The child should be able to always see the black circle on the ball as it moves around them (see Figure 7.3).

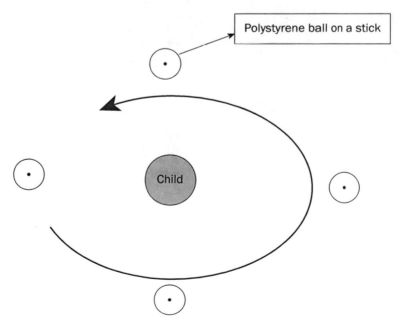

Figure 7.3 Modelling the orbit of the Moon

The phases of the Moon

During one lunar month (29 days and 12 hours), the illuminated part of the Moon changes shape to give the different phases of the Moon. A simple and visual simulation to illustrate how this happens can be achieved with an overhead projector and a polystyrene ball on a stick, again in a darkened room. This is best done with groups of four or five children at a time. You can say to the children that the overhead projector represents the Sun, they and you represent the Earth and the ball on the polystyrene stick is the Moon. Place the poly-styrene ball in front of the overhead projector slightly above head height and this position will illustrate the new Moon (you should warn the children of the dangers of looking at the overhead projector at this point). The child should then start to move the polystyrene ball on the stick anti-clockwise and they will see the waxing crescent, then the first quarter, then the waxing gibbous. When the polystyrene ball on the stick is opposite the projector they will see the full Moon. The child can then continue moving the polystyrene ball on the stick anti-clockwise to show the waning gibbous, last quarter and waning crescent. The cycle can then begin again with a new Moon (see Figure 7.4).

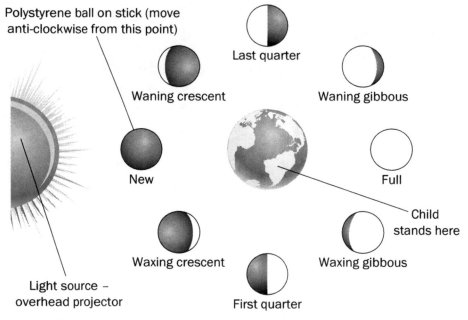

Figure 7.4 *Modelling the phases of the Moon*

You can encourage children to start keeping a lunar diary of the different phases of the Moon by observing the Moon in the evening, *Making careful observations (working scientifically)*. This is best done in the winter when it gets dark earlier. A further exercise to reinforce the different phases of the Moon is to ask the children to place cut-out phases of the Moon in the same order as the ones seen in Figure 7.5. This will also provide a useful assessment exercise for you of the child's understanding.

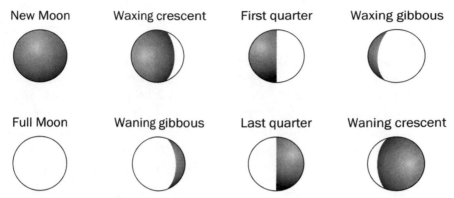

Figure 7.5 *Different phases of the Moon*

The Solar System

Children need to

> *describe the movement of the Earth and other planets, relative to the Sun in the Solar System.*

(DfE, 2013, page 170)

It is very difficult for us, let alone children, to fully comprehend the vastness of the Universe but children also find it difficult to understand what lies within what. There is often, for example, confusion between the Local Galaxy Group and the Solar System and which lies within which. Many children also have the geocentric view that the Earth is at the centre of the Universe and other heavenly bodies orbit around it.

The following activity, reminiscent of the Russian dolls which reside in each other, is useful in helping to understand what indeed lies within what, and begins to introduce the heliocentric alternative where the Sun is at the centre of the Solar System.

Ask the children to imagine that they are going to send a letter to a distant planet and ask them to write their own space address using the following words in their correct order: Solar System, Local Galaxy Group, Northern Hemisphere, England, Universe, Earth, Inner Planets, Milky Way, United Kingdom, Europe. Once the children have had a go at doing this, you can show the answers using a slide on the interactive white board.

Using video images of space to show that it is the Sun not the Earth that is at the centre of the Universe can also help to address this misconception. It is also an ideal opportunity for you to ask the children to find out the explanations of Ptolemy, Alhazen and Copernicus by using secondary sources of evidence such as books or internet sites, so they can understand how the geocentric model of the Solar System led to the heliocentric model which is accepted today as the correct scientific view. A useful assessment exercise for you to use is to give children statements of different people's views and ask the pupils to discuss the positives and negatives of such ideas to see if they agree on an explanation.

The planets

Another area of difficulty for children is remembering the order of the planets and then understanding their size and distance from each other. Children will primarily ask the question *Is Pluto a planet?* The following definition, which applies only to the Solar System, is that a planet is a body that orbits the Sun, is massive enough for its own gravity to make it round, and has 'cleared its neighbourhood' of smaller objects around its orbit. Under this new definition, Pluto and the other trans-Neptunian objects do not qualify as planets. You can help children remember the order of the planets by using mnemonics such as *My Very Earnest Mother Just Served Us Nothing* or they can have fun making up their own.

In order to help pupils fully appreciate the size and distance of the planets, you can ask the children to use this table of relative sizes and distances in the playground or their school field to model this idea. The sun could be a beach ball about 30cm in diameter.

Planet	Scaled planet diameter	Suggested model	Scaled distance from 'Sun'
Mercury	1mm	Poppy seed	12 metres
Venus	2.5mm	Peppercorn	23 metres
Earth	3mm	Dried pea	32 metres
Mars	1.5mm	Lentil	49 metres
Jupiter	30mm	Netball	167 metres
Saturn	26mm	Handball	300 metres
Uranus	10mm	Marble	About 600 metres
Neptune	10mm	Marble	About 900 metres

For some schools the modelling of Uranus and Neptune may be difficult; however it will illustrate the fact that the distances between the planets are vast compared to the sizes of the planets, and that the Solar System is mostly empty with planets only representing tiny amounts of matter in it. Your school might use a planetarium or orrery which can also help children visualise the order and motion of the planets around the Sun. They can then appreciate that the planets are spherical or nearly spherical in nature and they move around the Sun in a nearly circular or elliptical, anti-clockwise orbit and are held in orbit around the Sun by the Sun's gravitational pull.

CROSS-CURRICULAR LINKS

There are many opportunities to promote cross-curricular links with this scientific focus while also promoting literacy and numeracy. You can try out the following ideas when studying this subject.

Literacy

Literacy can be promoted by writing a diary while in space, a report of how you repaired the space station, factfiles on Ptolemy, Alhazen or Copernicus, book reviews of favourite science fiction texts, newspaper reports of a space launch or the Apollo 13 incident. You can also develop descriptive writing by exploring the world of aliens and work on pupils' debating skills by considering whether there is life in space. Books such as Jill Tomlinson's *The Owl Who Was Afraid of the Dark* (1998) or Martin Waddell's *Can't You Sleep Little Bear?* (2001) may also provide a starting point.

Numeracy

Numeracy can be promoted by looking at scaled versions of the planets in the Solar System and by looking at the passage of time and time zones around the globe.

Look at the use of different clocks through the passage of time, for example, stopwatches, stop clocks, water timers and digital timers which could also be created in design technology.

Other curricular links

This aspect of study can be used to develop the concept of explorer as a focus for a topic. It can provide you with many opportunities for design technology to design rockets and space-suits as well as other items of technology both now and for the future. You can consider things such as rainfall and wind speeds in both the UK and around the world and how this might compare to other planets. Music such as Richard Strauss's *Also Sprach Zarathustra* can provide you with the starting point of dance and drama, while space art and the work of Monet can provide a focus for the study of light.

HEALTH AND SAFETY

Remember when studying this topic to warn children of the dangers of:

- looking at the Sun directly;
- observing the Moon or the stars at night without a responsible adult;
- looking directly at the overhead projector during experiments.

Critical questions

» *On a scale of 1–10 (with 10 being completely confident), how confident do you now feel in your subject knowledge regarding Earth and space?*

» *Identify the specific area of the topic where you feel less confident and consider what other resources you might use to develop your confidence and subject knowledge.*

» *Consider how the use of models might help you teach some aspects of this topic to primary children.*

» *How might the internet further help you to teach this topic?*

Taking it further

ASE (2002) Earth and Space. *Association of Science Education*, PSR 72, April.

ASE (2007) Does the Moon Spin? *Association of Science Education*, PSR 97.

ASE (2009) Journeys into Space. *Association of Science Education*, PSR 108.

Osborne J, Wadsworth, P, Black, P and Meadows, JL (1993) *SPACE Research Report: The Earth in Space*. Liverpool: Liverpool University Press.

Websites

http://astroventure.arc.nasa.gov/DAP/

http://childrensuniversity.manchester.ac.uk/interactives/science/earthand beyond/phases.asp

www.cosmos4kids.com

http://downloads.bbc.co.uk/tv/guides/bbc_stargazing_live_activity_pack.pdf

www.e-education.psu.edu/astro801/content/l1_p3.html

www.esa.int/esaKIDSen/

www.fearofphysics.com/SunMoon/sunmoon1.html

www.fourmilab.ch/earthview/

http://hubblesite.org/gallery

http://nasa.gov/audience/forkids/kidsclub/flash/index,html

http://nasa.gov/home/index.html

http://theflatearthsociety.org/cms/

http://tycho.usno.navy.mil/vphase.html

http://video.nationalgeographic.com/video/kids/science-space-kids/solar-system-101-kids/

www.worldtimezone.com/

References

DfE (2013) *Teachers' Standards*. www.gov.uk/government/uploads/system/uploads/attachment_data/file/208682/Teachers__Standards_2013.pdf (accessed 17 February 2014).

8 Rocks

Introduction

Rocks is an area of science study which fascinates many children but, due to the length of geological time involved, there are many abstract and difficult concepts for them to understand. Since the formation of rock types is not easily observed, it is often difficult for them to understand the processes that have led to their creation. When you teach this topic you will be asking children to go beyond their concrete experiences of what they are handling and observing. It is through your skilful teaching of this subject that you may help them to start to understand and conceptualise how these simple objects have been forged by earth processes over time.

Rocks provide an enduring sense of interest for pupils from a very early age as they become aware of them in their immediate environment and when exploring their wider world. As children get older, the focus for your teaching can be extended to include the properties of different rock types, their uses, their composition and how physical processes have led to their creation over geological time. Children will start to observe and appreciate the benefits and limitations rocks have in our everyday lives. The fossils that are preserved in rocks provide opportunities for children to consider early life forms and how this might relate to other scientific topics such as evolution, as covered in Chapter 3. It is through a variety of creative activities, models, practical hands-on activities, as well as using secondary resources, that pupils will begin to explore and appreciate what at first glance may seem a very simple aspect of science for them.

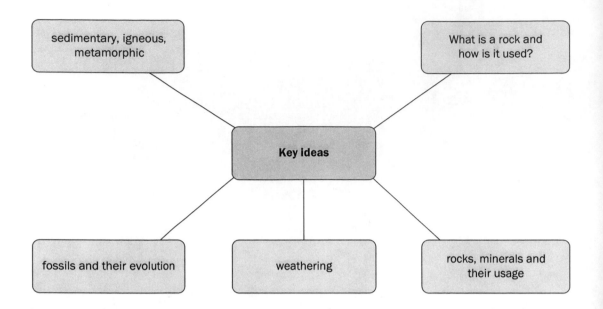

KEY VOCABULARY

The new national curriculum (DfE, 2013) stresses the importance of children using technical terminology accurately and precisely and building up an extended specialist vocabulary.

In Key Stage 1 children should begin to learn and explore the basic vocabulary to describe rocks that can be easily held and touched. It will mainly involve children becoming familiar with vocabulary to help them describe the texture of these materials, using words such as **rough**, **smooth**, **hard**, **soft** and **jagged**. Children should also be familiar with and learn vocabulary linked to the sizes of rocks such as **rock**, **stone**, **pebble** and **boulder**.

In Key Stage 2 pupils should begin to learn the basic vocabulary for the different kinds of rocks that are found on and under the Earth's surface, such as **igneous**, **sedimentary** and **metamorphic**. Children may already be familiar with the word **volcano** but will need to appreciate the difference between **lava** and **magma**. Children should start to become familiar with terminology such as **bedding** and **minerals**. They should be encouraged to name familiar rock types: **sandstone**, **limestone**, **chalk**, **marble**, **slate**, **pumice**, **coal**, **basalt**, **granite**, **gneiss** and **schist** as well as minerals such as **diamond**, **ruby**, **emerald**, **sapphire**, **quartz** and **amethyst**. Children should become familiar with the processes of **weathering** and **erosion** that wear down rocks over time. It is also important that they start to learn the difference between soils that are made of organic matter, such as **peat**, in contrast to those derived mainly from a rock type, such as **sandy soils** derived from **sandstone**.

Pupils should start to learn the names of simple creatures that have been fossilised in sedimentary rocks. These may include **trilobites**, **ammonites** and **dinosaurs**. Linked to this aspect of study, children should also become familiar with the terms **palaeontologist** and **palaeo-environment**.

CHILDREN'S IDEAS AND COMMON MISCONCEPTIONS

Your pupils may hold various misconceptions about how rocks were formed and how rocks differ. At an early age these may consist of the following:

- misunderstanding linked to what a rock is. Children will have limited ideas of where rocks are to be found, ie only on the surface of the Earth rather than deep underground, and they will think that the rocks beneath the Earth are just isolated fragments instead of understanding that they form layers of bedrock;

- a limited understanding of whether rocks are man-made or natural.

As children get older and move through Key Stage 2 the following misconceptions may still occur:

- children consider there is no difference in the origin of rock types such as igneous, sedimentary and metamorphic rocks;

- pupils will have a lack of understanding about the processes of weathering and erosion of rocks and will often only see these linked to human activities;

- though the children will have started to recognise that fossils occur, they will find it difficult to understand how different creatures will have lived in different ancient palaeo-environments, and how they have been trapped and preserved in sedimentary rocks;

- that fossils have evolved like other creatures over time;

- linked to the study of rocks, children often fail to understand that soils are made from rocks and organic matter;

- that the geology of an area will influence the soil type.

It is important that before you start teaching this topic you take time to find out about your pupils' levels of prior understanding so that it can help you focus your teaching and address any misconceptions that children may hold.

Topics and teaching strategies

What is a rock?

The new curriculum suggests pupils should be taught to:

- *identify and name a variety of everyday materials including ... rock;*

(DfE, 2013, page 149)

- *identify and compare the suitability of a variety of everyday materials, including ... rock.*

(DfE, 2013, page 153)

As children start to explore the world around them they will become familiar with the rocks that they find. However, children will at this stage consider rocks to be only of a limited size and when naturally occurring mainly rounded or jagged.

You can start to challenge these ideas by the skilful use of questioning and by encouraging children to make close observations of what they may have found (*working scientifically*). When talking to pupils you should encourage them to use the words rough, smooth, jagged and hard to describe what they may feel or have observed. Remember most children will consider the items they find are of natural origin. Try and get the children to question if their item is man-made or natural. Help them to look for clues such as very fine grain (like glass), unusual colours or smooth or flat sides indicating that the material has been processed, for example brick.

In order to help children to develop an awareness of the nature and use of man-made materials such as brick and concrete as well as that of rocks in their immediate environment you could send children on a materials trail around the school to record the location and use of such items. You could also encourage children to consider how these materials may have been used at home and get children to bring in pictures of these materials being used in order to sort them and maybe create a class collage.

Rocks in the landscape

Show the children a range of images of rock outcrops found within the landscape, ie mountains, hills and cliffs. Start to help them make links between these images and the rocks that they may have found. You could ask children to start collecting images, to use the internet to locate information about rocks in the landscape or draw pictures of where rocks might be found in the local environment. You should help the children to appreciate that their stones and the rocks in the landscape are linked and may have originated from a hill or quarry. Start to help the pupils appreciate that often in pictures there are large lumps of rock visible on the mountains and they are called boulders. You can ask the children to think about where these boulders may have come from in order to help them understand that mountains are constantly being eroded. This will help you to challenge their ideas about the permanent nature of rocks and should help them realise that such physical features and rocks are eroded over time. It will help them appreciate that rivers and seas also contain rocks and are involved in the processes of erosion and that the small rounded stones are called pebbles.

Ask pupils to draw what they think they would find if they were to go deeper and deeper into the ground and you may be surprised by the results. This will provide a useful means to assess pupils' understanding. It is likely that younger children will have very limited ideas about where rocks are found, often thinking that they are only located on the surface of the Earth. Most children fail to recognise that rocks are found in layers under the ground. Some think the Earth has a shell of rock around it very much like an egg and even when they know about rocks being found underground children often think these are isolated fragments, not linked together.

Though this is a difficult misconception to address, you can use children's first-hand experiences linked to home and school trips to help them reconsider their views about the concept of bedrock. Explore the ideas of quarries, sea cliffs and mines to help children appreciate the internal structure of the planet and consider that as they go deeper underground rocks form a continuous barrier in the earth.

Rock types

Children in lower Key Stage 2 will need to

compare and group together different kinds of rock on the basis of their appearance and simple physical properties.

(DfE, 2013, page 158)

In lower Key Stage 2 you need to help children understand that the term rock is a generic description for what is in fact a range of many different rock types which have a variety of origins. You will also need to get children to appreciate that very often the exterior surface of a rock is dull due to the process of weathering. While on some samples, most commonly limestone and sandstone, it may be possible to see the compositional feature of the rock you may have to ask children to break off a chunk of rock from their sample (using safety goggles, a small hammer and under your direction), to start to appreciate the nature and composition of un-weathered rock. Provide children with magnifying glasses and encourage them to describe what they can see on this new surface. Explain that rocks may be made of crystals, fragments of other rocks, fragments of fossils and may have a granular texture. Some rocks may also have lines in them which can indicate bedding planes, where the original silt or clay has been deposited in layers over time. Children will be excited if they think they have found gold in their rock. You should explain that gold is quite rare and that it is more likely to be the mineral iron pyrite (fool's gold). Such minerals have been deposited by mineral-rich waters percolating through the rocks. It is important for children to appreciate that rocks can vary greatly in weight due to their composition. To prove this to children, purchase a piece of pumice from a chemist and show the children that it will float compared to another rock type of a similar size. You can then go on to discuss with the children how pumice may have originated and how this may have helped it float.

FACTFILE

Granite is a hard, crystalline rock which may be found making up the hills and tors of Devon and Cornwall. It is an igneous rock formed by slowly cooling bodies of magma that are placed or trapped beneath the Earth's surface. Granite is used for monuments, shop frontages and gravestones due to its long-lasting nature and decorative qualities.

Pumice is also an igneous rock, formed when lava cooled very quickly above ground. It contains little pockets of air and is therefore light and will actually float in water.

Sedimentary rocks are rocks that have been formed by the erosion and deposition of another rock type or the skeletal remains of living creatures. Both limestone and sandstone are examples of sedimentary rocks.

Metamorphic rocks are formed when original igneous and sedimentary rocks have been 'morphed' to form this new rock type. This happens when these original rocks have been subjected to great heat and pressure deep within the Earth's core. Due to the high pressure exerted on these rocks the original layers of the rock can be distorted to give folds within the rock. Metamorphic rocks such as slate can be found in North Wales. Slate makes excellent roofing material due to the ease and thinness when splitting or cleaving it.

Studying rocks

Encourage children to consider the origins of features found within rocks. Ask them *Where have you seen grains like these before?* and *How did the crystals get into the rock and where have these fragments of shell come from?* Through careful questioning you will be able to tease out the concept of the origins of the three main rock types. This concept may well have been explored through geography topics and you should draw links between what they know in science and what they may have previously learnt.

Encourage children to think about how these different rock types are used by humans, making links to their physical properties. For example, granite is hard and unlikely to weather quickly so is used for tombstones, and slate is used for roofing because it is easy to split or cleave. Ask children to look at home and on the high street for the many uses of these different types of rock. Encourage pupils to take digital photographs of the rocks they have found, name them and label what they have observed about them so that a class collage can be built up around the uses of various rock types in their area.

Weathering

Through close observations children will start to recognise that rocks can be worn away and/or discoloured by the process of weathering over time. Though sometimes rocks are worn by humans, such as on a mountain track, many children will hold the misconception that it is always linked to human activities.

FACTFILE

Weathering is the name given to the process by which rocks are slowly worn away. This process may involve physical processes such as freezing and heating up the rock, or weather conditions such as wind and rain. Chemical weathering involves rainwater that has become acidic due to the absorption of CO_2 or pollutants from human activities. Biological weathering is a result of rocks being worn away by living organisms interacting with their surrounding material.

Ask children to find and draw examples of wear to both rocks and man-made materials, for example worn and cracked pavements and potholes in the road. Then discuss with children what may have led to this wear. Have they seen examples of rocks being worn or weathered in the natural environment? These might include cracks in rocks, plants growing in rocks, scree on mountains or rock falls under cliffs. It is important that children realise that the weather contributes to weathering and that this is a gradual process, unlike human activities, such as cutting, carving, splitting, grinding and crushing which are, in comparison, instantaneous.

To help children to further understand how the weather contributes to weathering the following investigations can be undertaken.

Get children to create a plaster of Paris or clay model (which has been fired) and ask them to think about whether this item will soak up water and, if it did, what would happen if it was frozen. (You could draw parallels with ice expanding in a bird bath.) Demonstrate how the material will absorb water and then put it in the freezer (it may need several freezings). Ask children to observe and discuss their findings (*working scientifically*). You could also place some vinegar or lemon juice on different rock types and again talk about the results (the acid will react with the limestone, fizzing and giving off CO_2 gas) This might link to discussions about reversible and irreversible changes in other science topics, ie materials (see Chapter 6).

To help children understand how wind action can lead to rocks being eroded, ask them to place strips of sticky tape outside around the school. Examine them and see what is being collected on them. They will be surprised to find bits of rock and soil attached. This could then be linked to a video of people sandblasting items and images of places such as Monument Valley. Finally, you could get the children to leave a sugar cube under a slowly dripping tap and record what happens to its shape.

FACTFILE

Plate tectonics is a theory which suggests that the surface of the Earth is covered by oceanic and continental plates and is like the skin of the planet. These plates very slowly move together or apart and are responsible for the creation of mountain chains such as the Andes, earthquakes and much of the volcanic activity found on the planet.

As children get older you should explain that the landforms and landscapes around us are linked to large-scale geological processes, rock types and the processes of weathering they have learnt about. You can model how folds are created and how mountains are pushed upwards by the movement of plate tectonics by asking pupils to place different coloured sheets of coloured modelling clay on top of each other and then push the sides together, as shown in Figure 8.1.

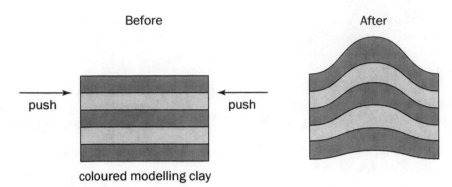

Figure 8.1 *Modelling clay folds*

Similarly, you can get children to layer flour and coloured sand in a plastic fish tank, move a sheet of wood sideways across the tank and observe what happens to the rock layers (see Figure 8.2).

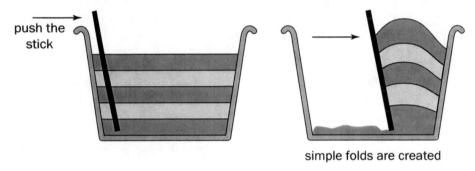

Figure 8.2 *Creating small-scale folds*

Fossils

Children in lower Key Stage 2 need to

> *describe in simple terms how fossils are formed when things that have lived are trapped within rocks.*
>
> (DfE, 2013, page 158)

It is a very exciting moment in a child's life when they spot a fossilised creature within a rock. Unfortunately, however, this fossil often represents only a fragment of the whole creature. Some fossils will be easy to identify, such as shells or fern leaves, but other creatures will be new to children. For this reason it may be necessary to use secondary sources to identify creatures such as trilobites, crinoids and ammonites (*working scientifically*). Some of these creatures will now be extinct and it is important that children start to appreciate that the fossils found in rocks provide a history of the evolution of life forms on this planet. Given this understanding you may now be able to liken the study of fossils by palaeontologists to the role of an archaeologist who reconstructs information about the past through evidence from old artefacts, buildings and earthworks. Palaeontologists can use the fossil record to find out about the creatures and their environments that existed long before humans in some cases.

You will need to explain that in a fossil the creature itself may have been turned to stone or that these items may be the real preserved remains of creatures, for example dinosaur bones.

Alternatively, what is found in the rocks may be an image or mould/cast of the creature after the creature itself has long decayed. To help pupils understand this concept you can make moulds and casts of fossils by getting a shell and placing it into modelling clay. Press the modelling clay in and around the shell and then remove it. This will leave the mould of an image of the shell in the modelling clay. Ask the children to fill this mould with liquid plaster of Paris and let it set. They can then peel back the modelling clay to leave a cast of the original shell. By undertaking this experiment pupils will start to gain an insight into the fossilisation process.

Often children do not make links between fossilised creatures and living creatures and you may need to explain that those creatures once moved, ate, reproduced and died. Show the children photos of fossilised dinosaur footprints, and compare with human footprints on a beach, or provide images of coprolites (fossilised dinosaur dung) or dinosaur eggs. This will help children to see that they really existed.

Soils

Children in lower Key Stage 2 need to

> recognise that soils are made from rocks and organic matter.
> (DfE, 2013, page 158)

You can start to get children to consider what is under their feet by asking them what they think is under the grass. Next ask children to dig a soil pit to provide a profile through the field soil so that they can see how the layers of organic matter, soil and rock fragments compose the soil under their feet. With this topic always remember to brief children on the need to work safely and to wash their hands if they are handling soil.

To further promote learning ask pupils to bring in soil samples in clear polythene bags from their gardens or immediate environments. Give them hand lenses to look closely at these samples and ask them to record their findings (*working scientifically*). You can use careful questioning to tease out what soil is made up of, whether soils are different or all the same and why we have soils. You can also challenge pupils to come up with suggestions for separating soils, for example sieves, meshes or colanders.

By providing children with different soil types, ie sandy, chalky and soil made from peat, you will encourage them to identify the different types of rock that may form part of the sample they are examining. It will also allow you to demonstrate that there are a range of soils found in the UK. This could lead you to thinking about how the geology of the UK varies and allow you to introduce the concept of a geological map of the British Isles.

The following investigation is also helpful in looking at the composition of soil. Ask children to dig up a sample of soil using a trowel. Provide them with a 1 litre, clear plastic bottle and lid and ask them to place the soil sample in it. When they return to class ask them to fill up the rest of the bottle with water and then screw the lid on tightly. The children should then shake it vigorously and leave it on a surface in the classroom overnight.

This investigation allows children to appreciate the variety of particle sizes in soil, as well as types of organic matter, for example grass clippings and roots that are often constituents of soil (see Figure 8.3). This could also link to work on materials and filtering.

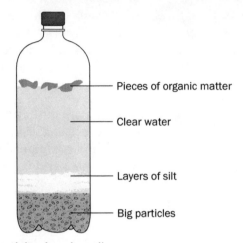

Figure 8.3 *Investigating particle sizes in soil*

Though children will be aware that soil contains mini-beasts such as worms, you should challenge them to consider why they are there. By setting up a class wormery (see Figure 8.4) as well as a composting bin outside, you can provide first-hand opportunities for children to observe, explore and examine (*working scientifically*) how organic matter is incorporated into soils and the valuable role worms and mini-beasts play in this process.

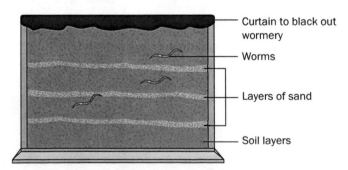

Figure 8.4 *A wormery*

Children will begin to understand that worms increase the amount of air and water in the soil and that they break down organic matter, for example leaves and grass, into nutrients that plants can use, and that they leave behind castings that are a valuable source of fertilizer for plants. Brandling worms are best known for the rapid processing of dead organic waste into nutrient-rich compost in a compost bin.

Evolution

In upper Key Stage 2 children will need to

> recognise that living things have changed over time and that fossils provide information about living things that inhabited the Earth millions of years ago.
>
> (DfE, 2013, page 173)

Through upper Key Stage 2, children should be made aware of the concept of evolution, and how the fossil record shows how animals adapted over time to meet the changing demands of the ancient environment they inhabited.

The dinosaur record will be familiar to children through media coverage, museums and a plethora of secondary sources. You can exploit this wealth of material alongside children's prior knowledge and fascination for this topic in order to discuss how animals have evolved to survive and thrive in ancient palaeo-environments.

FACTFILE

The tyrannosaurus rex, also known as T-rex, dominated North America during the late Cretaceous period (68–65 million years ago). The massive dinosaur's jaw was filled with huge, saw-edged teeth and it was a top predator feared by other dinosaurs.

The sabre-toothed tiger was a prehistoric animal which roamed the Earth with other prehistoric creatures such as the woolly mammoth. Sabre-toothed tigers could be found in mid-western US and areas of both North and South America. They received their names from the enormous canines they possessed which hung outside of their mouths.

Hominid refers to members of the family of humans.

Homo habilis was the earliest of our ancestors to demonstrate an important increase in brain size and was also the first to be found linked to the use of early stone tools.

Mary Anning was an early palaeontologist who found, collected and sold the fossils of prehistoric animals found on the Jurassic coast of Dorset around Lyme Regis. Among her many discoveries was the first identified ichthyosaur skeleton, which she found when she was only a child.

Charles Darwin was an English naturalist who realised that life had descended through time from common ancestors. He proposed that the pattern of evolution was a result of what he termed 'natural selection'. This meant creatures refined their existence over time due to their circumstances to best meet their survival needs. Darwin eventually published his theory of evolution in his 1859 book *On the Origin of Species*.

Alfred Wallace jointly published his theory of evolution by natural selection with Charles Darwin. Though Wallace was not overlooked during his lifetime and was awarded the Order of Merit, his importance in this field has been eclipsed by that of Charles Darwin.

Children can link the huge canine-toothed remains of creatures such as the sabre-toothed tiger and tyrannosaurus rex to their role as predators and carnivores at the top of their food chains. Similarly, discussions can be held about their style of movement, how they bred, whether they were warm or cold blooded, their speed and size and how scientists can use the fossil record to reconstruct information about these long-extinct creatures. It is also important that you discuss what has not been preserved and is a source of conjecture. For example, how did dinosaurs camouflage themselves, if at all, given that their skin colour has yet to be discovered.

By exploring the world of dinosaurs, for example, children can discover, through secondary sources, how palaeontologists such as Mary Anning helped people understand about ancient worlds. This should also be linked to Charles Darwin and Alfred Wallace who both pioneered work on early evolution by introducing the idea of natural selection. Encourage children to use secondary sources to find out about these individuals and perhaps produce a factfile or presentation on their contribution to our understanding of the past and science in general.

Human remains have also given us a relatively detailed account of our evolution, from our earliest ancestor Homo habilis who evolved around 2.3 million years ago, to the more recent Neanderthals and other hominids. Again though the fossil record is relatively complete much is yet to be learnt, speculated or deduced about the way our early ancestors lived, evolved and perished.

CROSS-CURRICULAR LINKS

Literacy

Literacy can be promoted through a variety of means. You can encourage children to research their favourite fossil or fossil type using the internet or non-fiction books. They can use this research to write a factfile about their fossil type, for example the ten deadliest dinosaurs or vegetarian or carnivore. You can encourage creative writing and writing reports using the concept of a 'Jurassic Park' type scenario. You can also encourage report writing by thinking, for example, about the day the world was hit by a meteorite.

You can encourage pupils' debating skills by considering whether we should bring back extinct species such as the sabre-toothed tiger or mammoth and whether it is fair on the creatures.

Numeracy

Numeracy can be promoted by looking at the concept of weight. Using scales pupils can compare rock weights, for example, pumice and granite. Pupils could be encouraged to consider geological time against a 12-hour clock scale to help them appreciate how small our existence on the earth has been.

Other curricular links

Rocks can provide you with many opportunities for design technology to design. You could get pupils using cookery to create their own rock types, for example Granite Scones, using a traditional scone recipe but including cherries, currants, raisins and mixed peel representing the composition of a granite or conglomerate. You can consider items such as rainfall and wind speeds in both the UK and around the world and how this might compare to other planets. Music such as Mendelssohn's *The Hebrides Overture (Fingal's Cave)* and Richard Strauss's *An Alpine Symphony* (linked to a person climbing up and down a mountain) can provide you with the starting point of dance and drama. Art may be promoted by thinking about Aboriginal art or ancient cave paintings such as in Lascaux and using different coloured soil types mixed with water to provide a paint or pigment. You can also purchase special marbling inks to create marbled paper.

HEALTH AND SAFETY

Remember when studying this topic to warn children of the dangers of:

- plaster of Paris or Modroc (plaster of Paris impregnated bandages) will become hot when mixed with water and is alkali; hence can be an irritant for individuals;

- when using clay wipe spillages off any surface and avoid making dust by rubbing on a hard surface to avoid inhaling the dust;

- if children need to hit a rock to get a clean un-weathered surface or to take a sample then only small hammers should be used along with safety goggles to avoid the risk of damage to eyes;

- wear gloves and/or wash hands thoroughly if examining soil samples. Mention the need for hygiene given the contaminant to be found in soil;

- when growing crystals, and considering the chemical change that happens when mixing baking soda and vinegar, children should be supervised when undertaking this work since both can prove an irritant to the eye and skin if they come into contact with individuals. Safety goggles should be worn alongside that of plastic disposable gloves.

Critical questions

» *On a scale of 1–10 (with 10 being completely confident) how confident do you now feel in your own subject knowledge regarding rocks as a topic?*

» *Identify the specific areas of the topic where you feel less confident.*

» *Where else might you look and what else might you do to develop your subject knowledge in those areas?*

» *What resources do you need to collect in order to successfully start teaching this topic?*

» *How might fieldwork visits be used to help enhance the study of this topic?*

Taking it further

Books

ASE (2010) *Be Safe in Science*, 4th Edition. Hatfield: ASE.

Dove, J (2002) *Geology and Art: Cross-curricular Links*. Available at http://onlinelibrary.wiley.com/doi/10.1111/1468–5949.00070/abstract (accessed 13 September 2013).

Howard, C (1987) A Method of Illustrating the Formation of Cross Bedding in Aeolian Deposit to Primary Children. *Geology Teaching*, 12(2), 68–9.

Howard, C (1989) The Value of Trace Fossils in the Primary Classroom. *Teaching Earth Sciences*, 14(2), 66–7.

Howard, C (1990) Flooding in a Local Context, for the Primary Child. *Teaching Earth Sciences*, 15(4), 106–7.

Websites

www.bbc.co.uk/nature/14343366 (accessed 6 February 2014).

www.letswasteless.com/cms/composting.aspx (accessed 6 February 2014).

http://news.bbc.co.uk/1/hi/8398451.stm (accessed 6 February 2014).

www.nhm.ac.uk/kids-only/dinosaurs/ (accessed 6 February 2014).

http://onlinelibrary.wiley.com/doi/10.1111/1468–5949.00070/pdf (accessed 6 February 2014).

www.outdoorclassrooms.co.uk/minibeasts-and-composting/minibeast-trapdoor.html (accessed 6 February 2014).

www.soil-net.com/primary/ (accessed 6 February 2014).

www.trilobites.info/trilobite.htm (accessed 6 February 2014).

References

DfE (2013) *Teachers' Standards*. www.gov.uk/government/uploads/system/uploads/attachment_data/file/208682/Teachers__Standards_2013.pdf (accessed 17 February 2014).

9 Light

Introduction

Light and the effects of light are noticed by many children from a very early age. As they get older, children will expect light from a candle to form part of their birthday celebrations and to be used for major celebratory events such as Christmas and Diwali. Light makes children feel safe from the dark and allows them to see items through their sense of sight. However, as children get older they will need to understand the detail and complexity of this subject. They will need to appreciate the difference between primary sources of light such as the Sun or a light bulb and secondary sources of light where objects are only visible because light is reflected off them, for example a fluorescent jacket or the Moon. When you teach this topic you will be asking children to go beyond their concrete experiences of seeing light to a conceptual understanding of its origins and how it travels through our Universe, to our world and from the Sun into their eyes.

Through skilful teaching of this subject you will be able to help pupils understand how something so simple and obvious as light is in fact rooted in very abstract and difficult concepts. It is therefore important that you use a variety of creative activities, models, practical hands-on activities and secondary resources to help pupils explore and appreciate this fascinating topic.

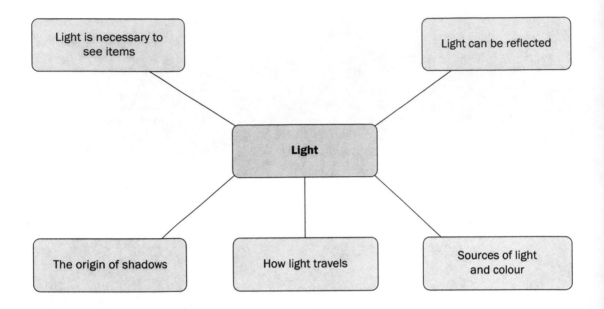

KEY VOCABULARY

The new national curriculum (DfE, 2013) stresses the importance of children using technical terminology accurately and precisely and building up an extended specialist vocabulary.

In Key Stage 1 children should explore the basic vocabulary to describe light. This should involve them becoming familiar with words which will aid their description of the properties of light such as **lighter, darker, dull** and **bright**. Children should also be familiar with the fact that **eyes** are responsible for the sense of sight.

In Key Stage 2 pupils should learn the basic vocabulary associated with light being **reflected** and **absorbed** and that humans use the properties of **reflected** light in equipment such as **periscopes** and **kaleidoscopes**. They should start to appreciate that light travels in **straight lines** and that it emanates from **primary** or **luminous sources** such as the sun and **secondary** or **non-luminous sources** such as light from mirrors. Children should start to realise that living creatures and non-living objects can emit light and **fluoresce**.

Pupils should learn how **shadows** are formed as a result of the **Sun's rays** being blocked and that humans use the **opaque, translucent** and **transparent** properties of materials to control the passage of light. Children will therefore start to realise that light reacts differently when it hits different surfaces and can be **reflected, diffused** or **refracted**.

It is also important that pupils realise that the light we see is only a small part of what is a wider **electromagnetic spectrum** that includes non-visible forms of light, including **radio-waves, microwaves, infrared, ultra-violet, X-rays** and **Gamma Rays**. Children should appreciate that the light we see, **white light,** can be split into its constituent parts, giving the colours of a **rainbow** (the **spectrum**) using a **prism**.

CHILDREN'S IDEAS AND COMMON MISCONCEPTIONS

From an early age children are aware of the sense of sight and that they see using their eyes. They may also understand that materials such as glass allow light into our houses. However, as children progress through Key Stage 2 the following misconceptions may occur. They often think that:

• light travels from our eyes to the source of light;

• not all light rays travel in a straight line since they can be bent;

• all objects are primary sources of light;

• light is not involved in how we see objects, since vision is linked to looking;

• light is not always necessary to see items and it can travel over great distances;

• shadows surround a person, since children don't understand what causes shadows;

• light travels through any medium in the same way as sound;

• light travels further at night;

• light is a single entity on its own and therefore unrelated to a wider spectrum.

It is important therefore that before you start teaching this topic you take time to find out about your pupils' levels of prior understanding to help focus your teaching.

Topics and teaching strategies

Early experiences with light

In the new curriculum at Key Stage 1 light, like sound, is not directly mentioned but it could be covered when investigating the senses since it suggests pupils should be able to

> identify, name, draw and label the basic parts of the human body and say which part of the body is associated with each sense.
>
> (DfE, 2013, page 149)

Through careful observations (*working scientifically*) and discussion you can help children to link the sense of sight and the organ they have for seeing, ie their eyes.

During this early age it is also important that children are given the opportunity to see which materials let light through, using items such as light boxes, plastic gels and Perspex. By undertaking such practical activities children can start to attribute simple properties to materials with regard to light. This allows them to, as the new curriculum suggests,

> identify and compare the suitability of a variety of everyday materials, including wood, metal, plastic, glass, brick, rock, paper and cardboard for particular uses.
>
> (DfE, 2013, page 153)

Sources of light

The new curriculum (DfE, 2013) suggests that pupils in Year 3 should be taught to

> *recognise that they need light in order to see things and that dark is the absence of light.*

> (DfE, 2013, page 159)

FACTFILE

Not all sources of light are primary sources of luminous light which emit light. They may be secondary, or non-luminous, sources of light where light is reflected or scattered off the surface of the object.

To assess how well children understand this, you could ask them to list sources of light they know, perhaps making an inventory of the sources of light in the classroom. Using these lists ask the children to categorise the light sources into natural and artificial. By discussing children's ideas regarding these light sources you will be able to quickly assess how well they really understand the concept of luminous and non-luminous sources of light.

To help children develop their ideas further, allow pupils to use a dark box, as shown in Figure 9.1. The interior of this box will stay dark unless light is let in through opening one of the small panels or if a light source is placed within the box. You can encourage children to place items such as a mirror, small torch, fluorescent material and a mobile phone into the dark box and see if they can predict (*working scientifically*) which items will light up the interior of the box, ie which are sources of light and which cannot be seen until light is allowed in from outside the box.

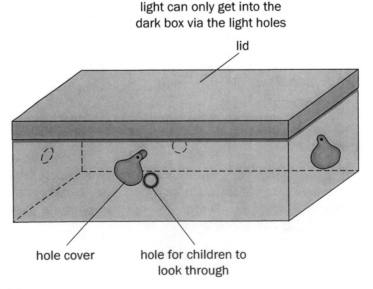

light can only get into the
dark box via the light holes

lid

hole cover

hole for children to
look through

Figure 9.1 *A dark box*

You can extend children's understanding of this topic by blacking out the classroom and challenging them again to think about which objects can be seen in the room and which cannot. Like opening a panel on the dark box, by opening the curtains children will be challenged to understand that items that are not light sources need a primary light source, such as the Sun, in order to be seen.

By doing these practical activities you can also draw out the fact that darkness is the absence of light. Ask children to think about where on Earth total darkness might be found. What about in space?

What is a shadow?

Once children have started to appreciate that darkness is the absence of light, this will naturally lead you on to a consideration of what causes shadows. As the new curriculum suggests, you should help children to:

- *recognise that shadows are formed when the light from a light source is blocked by a solid object;*

(DfE, 2013, page 159)

- *find patterns in the way that the sizes of shadows change.*

(DfE, 2013, page 159)

Children may already have started to consider the idea of shadows when studying the Earth and space (see Chapter 7). This allows children to study darkness in terms of day and night and seasonal change. It is now important that you help children understand how shadows are formed when light sources are blocked by opaque objects.

FACTFILE

A shadow is formed when the direct light from a light source is blocked by an opaque or translucent object. Since the light source is still illuminating the surrounding area the shadow appears dark. Scattered light still slightly illuminates the shadow area but the viewer sees this area as being black.

The umbra is the centre and darkest part of a shadow, where the light source is completely blocked by the opaque object.

The penumbra is the area on a shadow where some of the light source is blocked by the opaque object.

Ask children to draw pictures of what they think their shadow would look like on a sunny day. This will not only provide you with some formative assessment but also highlight any misconceptions they may hold, for example if a child draws a face on their shadow.

To develop understanding of the notion of shadows, allow children to create their own shadows in the classroom. Use card shapes and a light source, such as a light bulb in a desk lamp, which is smaller than the card shapes, as shown in Figure 9.2. Ask children to think about how the shadow is being created on the wall or the screen.

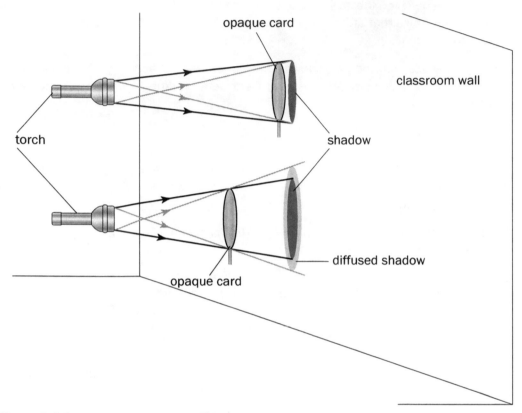

opaque card

classroom wall

torch

shadow

diffused shadow

opaque card

Figure 9.2 *Creating sharper and different size shadows*

You can get the children to investigate how the size of the shadow will alter when the card is closer to the lamp and when it is further away. Ask pupils to explain their ideas in order for you to assess their understanding of what is happening to create these shadows. You should encourage the children to realise that the closer the card is to the light source the more the light is blocked and hence the larger the shadow.

As well as the size of a shadow you can also ask children to consider whether the shadow's edge is sharp or fuzzy when it is bigger or when it was smaller. Using a light source which is considerably bigger than the card shape will help clarify children's thoughts with regard to this matter. It is important to tell the children to keep the angle between the card and light source constant during all these investigations in order to get reliable results (*working scientifically*).

Though not part of the new curriculum (DfE, 2013) you can relate the idea of the dark part of a shadow and the fuzzy grey area that can surround it to terminology such as the umbra and penumbra. Ask children to explain and draw what is happening when the card is near to the lamp and further away from it. They will soon realise that when the card is close to the screen there is little opportunity for the light rays from the light source to cross over before they hit the wall, hence there is a sharp shadow. In contrast when the card is closer to the light source the light rays can more easily cross each other and move apart which allows for a larger dark shadow, which not only has a less-defined edge but also has a diffused shadowy grey area surrounding it.

Children can be encouraged to experiment with shadows by creating their own shadow puppets. They can use the knowledge gained from the activities above to create sharp images on their puppet screens and puppets that appear to grow big and small during their productions.

This topic can be extended to focus on how shadows are formed on Earth using the natural source of sunlight provided by our Sun.

FACTFILE

The Sun formed over 4.5 billion years ago and is 93,020,000 miles or 150 million kilometres from Earth. The Sun's light takes about 8 minutes to reach the Earth with light travelling at approximately 186,000 miles per second or 300,000 kilometres per second.

When the Sun's rays hit the Earth they arrive at slightly different angles. This is due to the Sun being so distant and large compared to the Earth. These facts have implications for children's thinking with regard to how shadows are formed on Earth. Ask children to take their opaque-shaped cards outside and see what happens to the shadows when they hold them up in the air and close to the ground. Ask them if they changed size and did they still have fuzzy edges or sharp edges. Unlike the classroom investigations when the shadows of the same opaque-shaped cards changed size and had differing degrees of fuzziness, in sunlight the shadows that have been created will have only slightly fuzzy edges but more significantly will not have changed size. This is due to the distance and size of the Sun as a light source which provides little opportunity for the Sun's light rays to cross over before they hit items on the surface of the Earth.

As children get older you will need to revisit this work on shadows to meet the new national curriculum requirement to

> use the idea that light travels in straight lines to explain why shadows have the same shape as the objects that cast them.
>
> (DfE, 2013, page 174)

You may want to firstly revisit the earlier investigations but this time talk about what happens in terms of light travelling in straight lines. Get children to draw their predictions of how the light rays travelled from the light source via the object to create a shadow on the screen.

Can light be reflected?

In Year 3 children should

> notice that light is reflected from surfaces.
>
> (DfE, 2013, page 159)

Children may not be familiar with the word 'reflection' and some may confuse the idea of a reflection with that of a shadow.

FACTFILE

A reflection occurs when light bounces off the surface of an object. Very smooth and shiny surfaces easily reflect light giving a very clear image. Dull surfaces also reflect light but since the light rays are being scattered or diffused off their rougher surfaces the image may be harder to discern.

Ask children to investigate a variety of dull and shiny objects in a darkened room to see which surfaces light best shines off. Encourage children to draw what they think is happening in order to clarify their thinking and for you to assess their level of understanding so far.

There are many activities that can be devised as children get older to consider the properties of mirrors and what is happening to the light rays when they strike a mirror. However, at this relatively early age children should just be left to experiment with what mirrors can do with light. Ask children how to hold their mirror to see items or people behind them and ask them how mirrors are used in everyday life, such as in a car.

Light travels in straight lines

In Year 6, the new curriculum expects children to appreciate that

> light appears to travel in straight lines.
>
> (DfE, 2013, page 174)

Before you start any investigations linked to this concept get children to discuss where they may have seen rays of light coming from a light source and how they might have noticed that they travelled out from this light source. By getting children to think about car lights at night or even a laser beam they will quickly come up with the idea that light might actually be travelling in a straight line.

How light travels is in fact a difficult concept for children to comprehend and for you as a teacher to demonstrate, but what you can do is get children to investigate what effect light has as it travels in a straight line. It is also important that you consolidate this concept by linking how light travels to the sense of sight and how we as humans are able to see due to light rays entering our eyes.

FACTFILE

The structure of the eye

The cornea is the clear surface of the outer eye and it provides a barrier against germs and other damaging material entering the inner eye.

The iris provides colour to the eye from the genes of your parents. Its main purpose is to control the amount of light that is let into the eye. The pupil is the opening found in the centre of the eye. It allows light into the eye and changes its size as light levels vary.

During bright light the muscles of the eye contract causing the pupils (the opening at the centre of the iris) to shrink. During periods of poor light the muscles dilate which allows more light into the eye.

The lens is transparent and flexible and its curvature changes as a result of the muscles around the lens. By changing the curvature of the lens the eye is able to focus on objects it sees.

The retina is a sensitive layer of cells that lines the back of the inside of the eye. The retina changes images into electrical impulses that are sent to the brain by the optic nerve. This then allows the brain to make sense of what is seen. The two types of photoreceptors that comprise the retina are rods and cones. Rods enable us to see during low light levels while cones help us to see bright light and colours (see Figure 9.3).

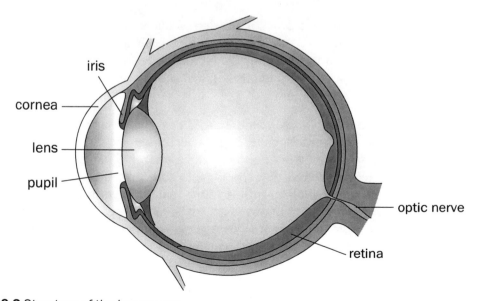

Figure 9.3 Structure of the human eye

At a simple level get children to sit in a darkened room and shine a very bright torch on to the wall. Then with the light shining, dust fine talcum powder in front of the torch so that the children can see that the beam of light is travelling out from the torch in a straight line. You can then ask them to describe and explain what they are seeing.

It is important that during this work on how light travels to clearly explain that, unlike sound, light does not need a medium to carry the rays through the air. This will complement the work on light in space where you talk about light travelling through the vacuum of space as it moves from the Sun to our Earth.

Once children have understood the idea that light travels in straight lines you can get them to make simple pinhole cameras, as seen in Figure 9.4.

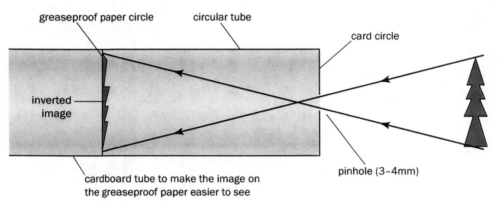

Figure 9.4 *A simple pinhole camera*

While making the pinhole camera it is worth drawing parallels with how this item works and the components of the human eye. You could say that the pinhole is like a simple iris, the card around it a simple pupil and that the greaseproof paper will act like a simple retina. You can talk to the children about what is missing and later on add a lens to help focus the images captured during this experiment.

When children have made their pinhole cameras ask them to look around at what they can see in strong daylight. Allow them to look at objects such as windows in the hall, trees outside or somebody stood in front of a door and ask them what they can see. Quickly children will be surprised and excited to note that the objects appear to be upside down on their screens. You will be able to show children this is the result of light travelling in a straight line. Light rays from the top and bottom of the object being viewed cross over as they pass through the pinhole, as shown in Figure 9.4, so that the light that came from the top of the image goes to the bottom of the camera and the light from the bottom of the image goes to the top of the camera.

Previous work on reflections and mirrors can be extended. Ask children to consider how we can get light to travel around corners. By providing mirrors and bright torches children will quickly work out how to angle the mirrors to reflect the light so that it may be seen. Get the children to make simple periscopes so that they can see light sources using two mirrors.

You can also look at the way light rays are bent or refracted in the medium of water. This can be investigated by putting a coin at the bottom of a large bucket. Then, using a long rod, ask the children to place its end on the coin. Children can also observe what the rod looks like when put in a large fish tank. Making ray drawings will help children to understand this notion.

How objects are seen

Older children need to:

- *use the idea that light travels in straight lines to explain that objects are seen because they give out or reflect light into the eye;*

- *explain that we see things because light travels from light sources to our eyes or from light sources to objects and then to our eyes.*

(DfE, 2013, page 174)

Children often hold the misconception that light travels from our eyes to the source of that light and that vision is linked to looking.

It is important that you challenge these ideas. Start by getting children to observe sources of light such as lit candles and torches (*working scientifically*) and then ask them to draw how they think these objects have been seen by our eyes by using straight lines to represent the light rays (this will reinforce the previous work you have undertaken that light travels in straight lines). To further develop these ideas ask children to draw directional arrows to represent light rays on simple concept drawings, as shown in Figure 9.5.

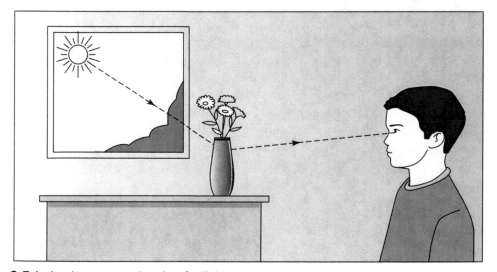

Figure 9.5 *A simple concept drawing for light rays*

Ask the children to discuss which direction the light comes from and where it is going. Be aware that children may start by drawing the light rays emanating from the eye to the light source or coming from the eye to the object and then to the light source.

Through your discussions you need to make sure that children understand that light sources send light rays in a straight line to our eyes. However, if the object is not a light source itself, light rays from a light source hit that object and they are then in turn reflected into our eyes so that the object can be seen.

What is colour?

Though the new curriculum (DfE, 2013) does not require children to investigate the creation and causes of colour, you should encourage children to study this aspect of light because it allows for a child's deeper conceptual understanding of the topic and helps them to understand how light is formed on our planet and the role of colour in the environment. The study of colour is also a very visually exciting and interesting topic for young minds to investigate and compliments other aspects of light that children are required to learn about under the statutory orders.

FACTFILE

Raindrops in the air act like tiny prisms to break up the daylight or white light into the spectrum, thus causing a rainbow. A rainbow displays all the colours of the spectrum which include red, orange, yellow, green, blue, indigo and violet.

You can introduce the idea of colour when looking at a range of phenomena which can include rainbows, colours on soap bubbles and the use of coloured gels and filters.

Children will be familiar with the concept of a rainbow from an early age but you should encourage them to realise that daylight or white light is made up of all the colours of a rainbow which should be referred to as the spectrum of white light. Children should also be urged to realise that seeing colours is as a result of surfaces reflecting certain colours, for example blue surfaces reflecting blue light. Filters produce a certain colour because they only let their own colour of light pass through them. This means that if pupils use a yellow filter only yellow light will be allowed through it hence making things appear yellow. If children put multi-coloured filters on top of each other then they will only see the colours that both filters allow through.

Encourage your pupils to consider the sorts of colours found in the wider environment and the reasons for them. For example:

- Why are wasps yellow and black?
- Why are berries red?
- If you see a red light what does that mean to you?
- How does colour affect your feelings towards the food you eat?

CROSS-CURRICULAR LINKS

There are many opportunities to promote cross-curricular links with this topic.

Literacy

Through extended pieces of writing children could be encouraged to use colour and light to convey mood in their written accounts. They could try to imagine what it would be like to have no sight and to be blind and convey their feelings in a report or through a play script. Poems, rhymes and alliteration could be written by children to convey what a sunny day, sunrise or sunset mean to them. Science fiction could also be used to get pupils to write about visiting a distant star and the adventures they might have trying to save the world as the blinding light of a dying Sun expands into a red giant ready to consume Earth.

Numeracy

Numeracy can be promoted by looking at the concept of time and how the length of daylight leads to clocks being altered to and from British Summer Time. Children can explore the role that colour plays in the construction of line, pie and bar graphs when displaying data as well as using measurements to map the changing length of shadows and angles to chart the height of stars within the night sky.

Other curricular links

Art provides a visual means of exploring the concept of light. Optical illusions created by artists such as Escher will provide a great visual challenge for children, while through the study of pointillism children can start to play with the optical properties of combining colour to create their own masterpieces. Through creating colour wheels or asking children to paint increasingly paler tones of single colours children will start to appreciate the hues found within nature as well as seeing what colours are needed to create new colours. Artists such as Monet and Caravaggio can also be examined in order to help children understand the role of colour and light in creating mood within their art.

Through combining their understanding of electricity with design technology children can start to explore lighthouses which flash to signal danger or make their own kaleidoscopes to help them further understand how mirrors reflect light. Further technology-based projects may lead to an investigation of other forms of light energy including radio waves, ultra-violet, microwaves, x-rays and Gamma rays.

HEALTH AND SAFETY

- Remind children never to look directly at the Sun or any other strong light sources such as bright lights;

- avoid glass mirrors where safer alternatives exist, such as plastic mirrors;

- children should not be allowed to use laser pointers while doing experiments for reasons of safety;
- if children suffer from epilepsy make certain you do not use flashing lights or strobes;
- warn children of the need to use light to avoid tripping in darkened rooms.

Critical questions

» On a scale of 1–10 (with 10 being completely confident) how confident do you now feel in your own subject knowledge about light?

» Identify the specific areas of the topic where you feel less confident.

» Where else might you look and what else might you do to develop your subject knowledge in those areas?

» What resources do you need to collect in order to successfully start teaching this topic?

» What artists might you like to study further to extend the theme of colour in this topic?

Taking it further

Books

ASE (2010) *Be Safe in Science*, 4th Edition. Hatfield: ASE.

Nuffield Primary Science: Key Stage 2 (1993) Light. London: HarperCollins Publishers.

Rutledge, N (2010) *Primary Science: Teaching the Tricky Bits*. Maidenhead: Open University Press.

Tomlinson, J (2005) *The Owl Who Was Afraid of the Dark*. London: Egmont.

Websites

www.bbc.co.uk/bitesize/ks2/science/physical_processes/light/play/ (accessed 6 February 2014).

www.bbc.co.uk/schools/teachers/ks2_lessonplans/science/see.shtml (accessed 6 February 2014).

www.primaryscience.ie/media/ds_centres/resources/17_light_materials_shadows.pdf (accessed 6 February 2014).

http://science.howstuffworks.com/nature/climate-weather/atmospheric/question41.htm (accessed 6 February 2014).

References

DfE (2013) *Teachers' Standards*. www.gov.uk/government/uploads/system/uploads/attachment_data/file/208682/Teachers__Standards_2013.pdf (accessed 17 February 2014).

10 Forces, motion and magnets

Introduction

As children develop they not only become familiar with the materials that surround them but also the forces that act upon these objects. Children initially see the physical effect of forces with objects falling from their grasp to the ground and they will also start to understand how exerting a force on an item may change its physical appearance. As children get older they will start to move beyond concrete experiences of forces to start to understand the abstract concepts involved. This will lead them to understand why objects float, why things fall to Earth and why things heat up when they encounter resistance to the forces acting upon them. It will also help children to understand that though forces cannot be seen they are constantly at work on Earth and affect our daily lives.

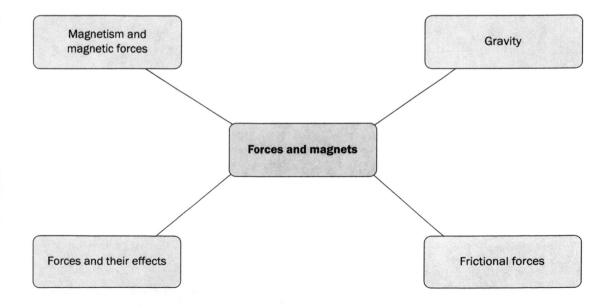

KEY VOCABULARY

The new national curriculum (DfE, 2013) stresses the importance of children using technical terminology accurately and precisely and building up an extended specialist vocabulary.

In Key Stage 1 children will start to see how the shape of solid items made from particular materials can be altered by **squashing**, **bending**, **twisting** and **stretching** them. Forces may also be seen in terms of **pushes** and **pulls**.

In Key Stage 2 you should continue to develop pupils' vocabulary to include an understanding of magnetism.

Children should be introduced to the major force that affects our Earth, that of **gravity**, and should start to discover the difference between **mass** and **weight**. They can be shown that other forces are evident in our daily lives which lead to **air resistance**, **water resistance**, **drag** and **friction** that act between moving surfaces. Children will start to realise that the reason some objects **float** or are **buoyant** is due to the **upthrust** they experience once placed in water. This leads on to the idea of **reaction forces** that have an equal and opposite reaction. They should be shown how we can overcome forces in our daily lives through mechanisms such as **levers**, **pulleys** and **gears**. Pupils will be taught how we measure particular forces in the classroom using a **force metre** in units called **newtons (N)**, and they can be encouraged to find out about famous scientists linked to this topic, such as **Galileo Galilei, Archimedes** and **Isaac Newton**.

Children should start to appreciate that magnets have both a **north** and **south pole** and that opposite poles **attract** while similar poles **repel** each other. **Magnetic forces** can act over a distance and through items. By testing items with a variety of magnets such as a **horseshoe** or **bar magnet**, pupils will see that not all materials are magnetic.

CHILDREN'S IDEAS AND COMMON MISCONCEPTIONS

During the study of this topic children may hold various misconceptions about how forces are caused and how they act on objects and humans. At an early age these may consist of the following:

- confusion between what is a push and a pull;
- that forces are needed to get items moving or to change their direction;
- associating movement with an object, such as a car;
- forces can change the shape of objects.

As children progress through Key Stage 2 the following misconceptions may still occur:

- objects float or sink due to a particular property they have;

- all heavy objects sink;
- resting objects have no forces acting upon them;
- objects fall because humans let go of them;
- the heavier the object the quicker it will fall;
- air causes objects to fall or stops items from falling;
- confusing kilograms with units of force (newtons);
- forces are seen as separate rather than paired;
- forces that act in pairs are always equal and opposite;
- friction is associated with objects such as wheels on a bike and is linked to grip;
- friction does not necessarily slow an item down;
- air resistance is solely linked to the air moving;
- gravity is only found on Earth;
- gravity becomes stronger the higher off the ground you are.

Linked to the study of magnets in Key Stage 2, pupils may think that:

- all metals are magnetic;
- there are no natural magnets;
- magnets are somehow responsible for objects sticking to them;
- all magnetism is permanent.

Topics and teaching strategies

Early experiences with forces

In the new curriculum at Key Stage 1 forces are not directly mentioned but could be covered when investigating the uses of everyday materials, since it suggests pupils should be able to:

> find out how the shapes of solid objects made from some materials can be changed by squashing, bending, twisting and stretching.

> (DfE, 2013, page 153)

Give young children a variety of materials such as modelling clay, rubber bands and sponges and ask them to describe what happens to each of these materials when they push or pull them.

Through careful observations (*working scientifically*) and discussion you can help children to link the creation of a variety of everyday objects to forces applied to particular materials, such as the bending of metal to make cars. Start to encourage children to realise that forces are all around us. Ask the children to list daily life forces, such as opening doors, by going around the classroom labelling where these forces need to be applied. Encourage them to take part in activities that use forces such as rolling objects down a slope, ball games during physical education and action songs such as *Row, Row, Row Your Boat* in order to feel the effects of forces.

At this early age it will be enough for children to understand that forces can be seen in terms of pushes and pulls. Since these terms can be difficult for some pupils to remember help them think in terms of 'pulling towards them' and 'pushing away from them' to embed this vocabulary.

Remember that pupils cannot see a force – they can only see its effect – and this makes it a difficult concept for young children to grasp. Therefore, the study of forces will need to be revisited in Key Stage 2 alongside the concept that some forces cannot be felt.

The effect of forces

The new curriculum (DfE, 2013) suggests that pupils in Year 3 should be taught to

> *compare how things move on different surfaces.*
>
> (DfE, 2013, page 160)

During early Key Stage 2 the focus of your activities should be on the effect of forces. Ask children to collect images of items that move and to organise them by their means of propulsion. Ask them to investigate whether they will move differently on different surfaces. This will allow you to assess their current understanding of forces and the effects surfaces have upon moving objects. For example, get children to roll similar cars down ramps. Tell the pupils to keep the angle of the ramp constant but vary the surface of the ramp using sandpaper, shaggy carpet, plastic and a variety of liquids such as water, oil and grease. Before the start ask them to predict how the car will react to each different surface and to gather and record their data (*working scientifically*). Children can use a variety of labelled diagrams with keys and bar charts to display and present their findings to others. You can also ask pupils to group materials by the way they make the car react (*working scientifically*).

Gravity

Year 5 pupils should be taught to

> *explain that unsupported objects fall towards the Earth because of the force of gravity acting between the Earth and the falling object.*
>
> (DfE, 2013, page 170)

Though many children may have heard of gravity they are likely to have only a limited understanding. They should be encouraged to understand that gravity is directional and doesn't just act on the Earth.

FACTFILE

Gravity is the force that makes things fall to the ground on Earth as well as other planets. It is responsible for holding the Earth and the other planets in their orbits around the Sun.

All objects attract one another due to their masses (how much matter there is in something). Due to the enormous mass of the Earth and its distance from other objects, the force of attraction between it and other items is measurable. Forces can be measured using the unit of newtons (N). How much the Earth pulls on an object is called its weight and since weight is the force exercised by gravity weight can be scientifically measured in newtons. 10 Newton (10N) is roughly equal to the force of the Earth's gravity acting on 1,000 grams or 1kg of mass.

Sir Isaac Newton was an English physicist and mathematician born in 1643. He is remembered most for his work on the laws of motion and gravity. In 1687, Newton wrote a famous book called the *Philosophiae Naturalis Principia Mathematica* in which he outlined his theory of universal gravitation and his three laws of motion.

Galileo Galilei was born in 1564 near Pisa in Italy. He created one of the earliest telescopes and made many discoveries about our Solar System. He discovered that Jupiter had four moons which orbited it thus showing not everything orbited the Earth. These discoveries along with his support of the Copernican theory that the Sun was at the centre of the Solar System got him into a lot of trouble with the Catholic Church of the time.

Children may have started to understand gravity while studying the Earth and space. They may know that an apple falling to the ground is falling towards the Earth's centre.

Though gravity is a very abstract concept for children you can extend their current knowledge of this force acting on objects falling to the ground by getting them to find examples from their own lives and from secondary sources, such as the internet, where gravity may be seen to act. Ask children to find examples of gravity acting from their own life and from secondary sources such as the internet. They could draw pictures to explain how gravity acts on a ball thrown into the air. Encourage pupils to think about gravity on the Moon. For example, what effect does it have when the force of gravity is reduced when astronauts are in space? Use video clips to reinforce this idea once you have discussed the concept of reduced levels of gravity such as on the Moon.

Though the topic of gravity is complex for children to understand it is important that you make children aware that gravity is not the only force at work on static objects. There is an opposite or reaction force at work too. As Newton's third law of motion suggests, *for every action there is an equal and opposite reaction*. For example, if a vase is placed on a table, the Earth pulls the vase down on the table (its weight) while the vase also pulls the Earth upwards with an equal and opposite force (though the Earth's mass is too large for us to notice any perceptible change).

Frictional forces

Older children will need to start to understand how forces interact with the objects they are acting upon and how this can be used by humans for their own benefit. The new curriculum states that children in Year 5 should

> identify the effects of air resistance, water resistance and friction, that act between moving surfaces.

> (DfE, 2013, page 171)

Friction

Pupils need to thoroughly understand the concept of friction in order to appreciate what is happening when it comes to air and water resistance.

FACTFILE

When an item moves against another item, it encounters frictional forces. Friction makes it harder for things to move since there is a force acting in the opposite direction to the object's movement.

When objects move through air and water this movement is resisted by an opposite, equivalent, frictional force from either the water or air. This is called air or water resistance. Parachutes, planes, bikes and cars all experience resistance as they move. The faster the item moves, the bigger the resistant forces become.

A very quick activity to start your work on friction and to generate discussion about this idea is to get children to place their palms together and to quite quickly rub them back and forth. Children will tell you that their hands start to feel hot. Ask them to consider what is causing this heat and they should conclude that it is the opposing movements of their rough palms.

Next ask children to try and unscrew the smooth lid on a plastic jar which has been tightly secured. Get them to try first with wet hands, then with dry hands and finally wearing rubber washing-up gloves. Again ask them to consider which made opening the jar the easiest and why. Many children will start to use the word 'grip' and it is important that you encourage them to use 'friction' instead.

At this point you can revisit and extend the car on the ramp experiment or alternatively children can attempt to move wooden blocks on a variety of flat surfaces, such as plastic, rough sand paper and carpet, as shown in Figure 10.1.

Increased frictional forces mean that more force is needed to make the wooden block move. This experiment will also help children appreciate that more than one force is involved in such situations. The pulling of the elastic band generates a pushing force which acts upon the block. This push from the elastic band starts to increase the friction between the board

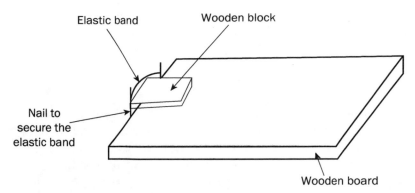

Figure 10.1 *Moving a wooden block on a variety of flat surfaces*

and the base of the block. If these two forces are balanced the block will stay still. However, if the push from the elastic band is greater than the frictional force then the block will move. Pupils will also realise that friction cannot happen if there is no movement between different surfaces. Encourage them to draw annotated diagrams to record and describe what is happening in this investigation as a means for you to assess their understanding.

Further challenge pupils by asking them to add additional weights on the block and to predict whether they will need a greater force to move the blocks along the board. Similarly, how might they make it easier for the block to be moved, and what would happen if they added wheels?

FACTFILE

Scientists use a force meter to measure a force. They contain a spring connected to a metal hook and when a force is applied to the hook the spring stretches. The bigger the force applied, the longer the spring will stretch, thus giving a higher reading. Forces are measured in newtons (N).

You can introduce a force meter to pupils to help them quantify the forces that are being applied to make the block move. By attaching the force metre to the elastic band and pulling the band with the force meter the children will be able to see how much force has been applied to the block. This will not only make for a much more accurate comparison of the forces that have been applied but will also allow pupils to accurately record and display the data gathered in this investigation (*working scientifically*).

Once children have gained an understanding of friction you can get them to think about the real-life benefits and drawbacks of friction. Using a bike you can demonstrate how the brakes apply friction to the wheel to slow it down. You can ask children to use secondary sources (*working scientifically*) to gather other examples of the benefits of friction and to find surfaces which provide reduced levels of friction. You can also challenge pupils to design the best sole for a trainer to stop the wearer sliding about.

These investigations have so far focused on friction between two solid surfaces but friction can occur when a solid object moves in water, leading to water resistance, and when a solid surface moves in air, involving air resistance.

Water resistance

Start by asking if pupils have been or have watched sailing and ask them to describe any forces that might be involved. Then ask the children to design and make their own simple sailing boats using flat pieces of wood or flat-bottomed plastic trays, dowels and paper or fabric for sails. They can test what happens to their boats in a water bath when they blow on the sail. Discuss what force is stopping all their blowing energy from allowing the boat to move even quicker through the water. It is important that you talk about the frictional force between the boat's hull and the water in terms of water resistance or drag.

FACTFILE

When a boat moves through water it pushes a large number of water molecules out of the way leading to a disturbance in the water. Similarly, when a plane flies through the air it pushes a large number of air molecules out of the way and causes a disturbance in the air. Both actions slow down the objects by a small amount leading to what is referred to as drag.

Archimedes was a Greek mathematician and inventor. He was famous for describing the principle of the lever and the hydraulic screw (Archimedean screw). Linked to the concept of floating and sinking he is most noted for discovering that if an object is immersed in a liquid it loses weight equivalent to the weight of the amount of liquid it displaces.

Challenge pupils to think about what will happen if they change the shape of their hulls, or if they add a load to the boat. You could even get children to compare the movement of the boats through a variety of liquids such as milk, cooking oil and double cream to see if the thickness of the liquid will affect the drag. Children can use force meters to quantify the force needed to pull their boats through a variety of liquids in order to collect, analyse and display their data (*working scientifically*).

While studying water resistance it is also worth exploring why some objects float given their obvious weight and the force of gravity acting downward upon them. Start this work by getting children to make different sized and shaped boats out of modelling clay or tin foil and ask them to try and work out which shape of boat will float and carry the most weight.

Next ask pupils to weigh a brick using a Newton meter in the air and then in a deep bowl of water. Children will be surprised to see that the water has seemingly made the brick lighter. With help children will realise that though the force on the brick has stayed constant, the brick is now being supported by an upthrust from the water. As Archimedes discovered, this phenomenon is linked to the volume of water displaced by the object. Children can be helped to experience upthrust by placing a ball into a large bath of water and trying to push down on to it. They will feel the upthrust on the ball as it is pressed into the water and can observe the water level rising in the bath.

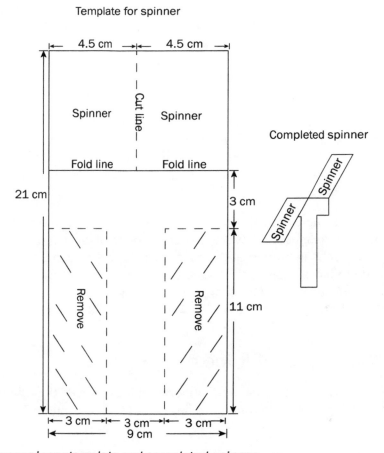

Template for spinner

Completed spinner

Figure 10.2 *Paper spinner template and completed spinner*

Air resistance

You can develop children's ideas about air resistance using a variety of fun activities. Using paper spinners, as shown in Figure 10.2, you can get children to discuss which factors are responsible for stopping the spinner from falling. Using a variety of papers, altering the size of the 'wings' and adding weight in the form of paperclips to the spinner you can further challenge children's thinking about this notion.

It is important that you introduce the terminology of air resistance or drag to accurately describe this idea.

You can further develop this idea by discussing the use of parachutes to stop objects falling too quickly. Pupils can create a model parachute using sticky tape stuck on to the corners of a 30cm-square piece of plastic, with a 15cm-long piece of string from each corner, suspending a given weight such as 10g from the strings. This should be dropped from a fixed height. They should draw and describe what is happening with the forces in this experiment.

Children should realise that the weight is too much for the parachute so it falls quite quickly under the force of gravity. If they repeat the experiment using 2g weights the parachute will fall more slowly. Initially the weight was greater than the air resistance provided by the parachute and hence the speed of fall was quick, while the drag provided by the parachute on the second occasion was greater than the weight and hence the fall was slower. Using this experiment also provides a good opportunity to explore the idea of unbalanced forces.

You can challenge children to think about changing other variables such as the shape of the canopy and types of materials used in this experiment and to observe and predict what will happen (*working scientifically*). You can also ask pupils to consider if nature provides natural types of parachutes to help stop animals from falling quickly to Earth such as flying squirrels or sycamore and dandelion seeds.

At some point explain to children that if two objects such as a stone and a 10p coin are dropped from the same height and have no resistant forces acting upon them they will fall at the same rate and reach the ground at the same time, as suggested by the work of Galileo. Though this is hard to prove experimentally, selected science video clips, such as YouTube's *Misconceptions about Falling Objects*, may help. Challenge pupils to think about what would happen if they were to drop two items on the Moon – would they fall to the ground as they would on Earth?

Reducing the effects of forces

Once pupils in upper Key Stage 2 have an understanding of forces they should think about how they might overcome forces in their everyday lives. As the new curriculum suggests, they should

> *recognise that some mechanisms, including levers, pulleys and gears, allow a smaller force to have a greater effect.*
>
> (DfE, 2013, page 171)

Sometimes frictional forces are too difficult for humans to overcome, such as opening a tin or undoing a wheel nut, so a knowledge of the means of transferring forces is important.

Encourage children to think of examples of when objects are difficult to move due to the large forces necessary, such as a nail in wood. How might they change a small force into a larger one to remove the nail? Demonstrate how the use of a simple lever such as a claw hammer can achieve this. Other examples could include using a screwdriver to open a lid or a wheelbarrow to lift a heavy load. Similarly, pulleys enable heavy loads to be raised with little effort. A simple example is throwing a rope over a tree branch as a means of lifting a weight.

Though it is difficult for children to be involved with practical activities linked to pulleys, you can discuss and examine their uses in everyday life. For example, children may have come across buckets being pulled up from a well, and you could examine how a pulley makes this possible. Think about the way a pulley is used to raise a flag up a flag pole, how they are used to pull up classroom blinds or even used by rock climbers to keep them safe.

Some pupils in their studies will have seen or know or have learnt about water wheels, and these will provide an excellent discussion point to consider how pulleys can also be used to change the direction of motion from the moving water to the grindstone, to increase or decrease the speed of a shaft, or to lift the sacks of flour once milled.

This work will lead naturally to the study of gears, which transmit forces through rotary motion. Children may have come across this idea through their bikes so you can use this as a starting point to discuss how such gear systems work. Encourage children to observe how a change of speed is achieved by putting together gears which have different numbers of teeth on them. Bring an old-fashioned hand whisk into school to illustrate this more easily.

Children can develop their knowledge of gears by experimenting with commercial gear kits that are now available, but they will also have great fun creating their own gearing systems to help give motion to items created in design technology lessons.

Magnets and their forces

To complement the study of forces, children in Key Stage 2 should be given the opportunity to learn about magnets and the forces associated with them. Year 3 pupils should:

- *notice that some forces need contact between two objects, but magnetic forces can act at a distance;*

- *describe magnets as having two poles;*

- *predict whether two magnets will attract or repel each other, depending on which poles are facing them.*

(DfE, 2013, page 160)

Let pupils experiment with a variety of magnets such as bar, ring, button and horseshoe magnets. They will realise that magnetic forces, unlike most other forces, can act without direct contact. By getting children to place a paperclip under a book while holding a magnet on top they will be able to see how magnetic forces can pass through solid materials. They could also investigate if magnetism works through water in a similar way or test the distance over which such magnetic forces operate by seeing how far away from a paperclip a magnet can be held before the paperclip is pulled towards it. Children can compare the strength of a variety of magnets and can display this data in tables (*working scientifically*).

FACTFILE

Magnets are items that produce an invisible magnetic force called a magnetic field. Iron filings when used safely can show the magnetic field around a magnet. Though iron is attracted to a magnet, other metals such as silver, gold, copper and aluminium are not. Non-metals such as plastic and wood are also not attracted to a magnet.

Through practical experimentation with a bar magnet children will notice that one end of the magnet, which is usually painted red (the north pole), will repel another red end. This repulsion of like poles is similarly true for the blue ends (the south poles). However, the blue end will be attracted to the red end. When discussing this phenomenon with the children remember to use the correct vocabulary. Challenge pupils to arrange a row of bar magnets on a table so that they either all stick together or cannot be stuck together to assess their understanding of this subject.

To extend pupils' knowledge get them to research a range of uses for magnets in everyday life, for example magnets on cabinet doors, a magnetic paperclip holder and refrigerator magnets.

Magnetic materials

Children in Year 3 will also be required by the new curriculum to:

- *compare and group together a variety of everyday materials on the basis of whether they are attracted to a magnet, and identify some magnetic materials;*

- *observe how magnets attract or repel each other and attract some materials and not others.*

(DfE, 2013, page 160)

Ask pupils to sort a range of metallic and non-metallic objects into these groups. They will quickly learn that magnets are attracted to metals, but you must also make them realise that not all metals are magnetic. Get pupils to try and pick up a piece of aluminium using a magnet or even a gold ring to demonstrate this.

FACTFILE

Just three metals are in fact magnetic: nickel, cobalt and iron. If an item is an alloy (mixture) of any of these elements then it will become magnetic. Magnetite is a mineral ore of iron and forms a naturally magnetised rock, often referred to as a lodestone.

Though not explicit in the new curriculum (DfE, 2013), children should also be encouraged to realise that if a magnet is attracted to a metal object, then that metal itself may be turned into a magnet. It is magnetised. Ask pupils to stroke a bar magnet along a paperclip or nail which originally was not magnetic to show how these objects now retain this magnetic force.

CROSS-CURRICULAR LINKS

There are many opportunities to promote cross-curricular links when studying this topic.

Literacy

Through extended pieces of writing, poetry and rhymes children could be encouraged to describe what it is like to feel forces they might encounter, for example when on a roller coaster. Science fiction could also be used to get pupils to write about special powers which can help them lift heavy items thus defeating the power of gravity.

Numeracy

Numeracy can be promoted by looking at the concept of measurement linked to reading a force meter or by using timers to record the speed of objects falling. Children can record these measurements and display the data using line and bar graphs.

Other curricular links

Children can be encouraged to express natural magnetic fields such as the Northern Lights through art or to listen to music such as Holst's *The Planets* to feel elemental forces of the Universe conveyed in sound. Through the study of historical features such as Stonehenge and the pyramids children can be encouraged to consider how these large stones were moved by humans using simple gears and pulleys. Through combining children's understanding of magnetism and forces with design technology children can create their own gear and lever systems to make items move.

HEALTH AND SAFETY

Remember when studying this topic:

- use sealed containers to examine magnetism with iron filings;

- do not use small magnets that young children could swallow;

- make certain the magnets do not pinch;

- keep magnets away from electronic circuitry;

- use low loads when testing;

- warn of dangers of getting too close to mechanical gear systems;

- warn children of the need to be safe when applying forces to objects and to wear eye goggles if needed;

- children should not stand on unsafe or high surfaces to test forces.

Critical questions

» On a scale of 1–10 (with 10 being completely confident) how confident do you now feel in your own subject knowledge of forces and magnetism as a topic?

» Identify the specific areas of the topic where you feel less confident.

» Where else might you look and what else might you do to develop your subject knowledge in those areas?

» What resources do you need to collect in order to successfully start teaching the topics of forces or magnetism?

» In particular, what video clips could be watched or visits arranged to further understanding of gears and pulleys?

Taking it further

Books

ASE (2010) *Be Safe in Science*, 4th Edition. Hatfield: ASE.

Cross, A and Bowden, A (2009) *Essential Primary Science*. Maidenhead: Open University Press.

Websites

www.bbc.co.uk/bitesize/ks2/science/physical_processes/forces/quiz/q74052238/ (accessed 5 February 2014).

www.bbc.co.uk/bitesize/ks2/science/physical_processes/forces/read/1/ (accessed 5 February 2014).

www.bbc.co.uk/schools/scienceclips/ages/10_11/forces_action.shtml (accessed 5 February 2014).

www.nuffieldfoundation.org/primary-science-and-space (accessed 5 February 2014).

References

DfE (2013) *Teachers' Standards*. www.gov.uk/government/uploads/system/uploads/attachment_data/file/208682/Teachers__Standards_2013.pdf (accessed 17 February 2014).

11 Sound

Introduction

Children from an early age become familiar with the sounds in the environment and learn through experience to react to them. From the earliest sounds of a rattle in a cot to the more complex sounds that are conveyed by music, children learn to listen to these sounds and, as they grow older, interpret them. Through their sense of hearing they can discriminate between the loudness and pitch of a sound and locate its source. However, as pupils get older they will have to start to understand what causes sound, how it is heard and how it travels through the air and other mediums in order to extend their learning. These may prove difficult ideas for children to comprehend since they have yet to understand the abstract ideas that underpin this scientific phenomenon.

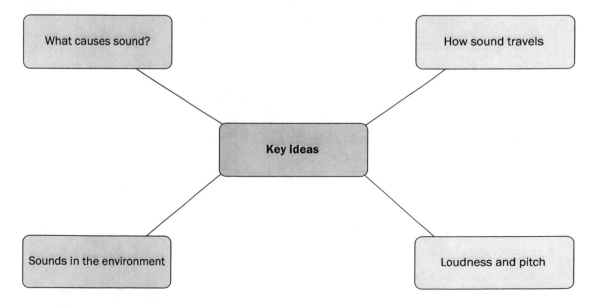

KEY VOCABULARY

The new national curriculum (DfE, 2013) stresses the importance of children using technical terminology accurately and precisely and building up an extended specialist vocabulary. Therefore it is important that when you teach this topic you seek to introduce new terminology in order to extend pupils' existing vocabulary.

In early Key Stage 1 children should begin to learn and explore the basic vocabulary linked to describing contrasts in the sounds they can hear, such as **soft** and **loud** sounds. They should also be able to name an **ear** in order to identify the organ responsible for the sense of hearing.

In Key Stage 2 pupils should begin to learn the basic vocabulary associated with identifying the processes that create sounds. They must start to realise that **vibrations** generate sounds and that sounds need to travel through a variety of **mediums** such as air. Pupils should start to refer to the **frequency** of the vibrations and how the **pitch** of a sound represents a range of high or low **notes**. The loudness of a sound **source** is referred to by its **volume** and that sound may be measured in **decibels**. Since some sounds would be unbearably loud unless we tried to reduce their loudness children should be familiar with words such as **insulation** and **ear-muff** or **ear-defenders**. Given that sounds may bounce back off surfaces they must be familiar with the idea of an **echo** and that animals use **echo location** and humans use **sonar** in order to locate objects using sounds.

CHILDREN'S IDEAS AND COMMON MISCONCEPTIONS

Pupils may hold various misconceptions about the sources of sound and how sound travels to reach our ears. At an early age these may consist of the following:

- sound is always present inside our ears;

- sounds are only present if they can be heard by a child;

- a sound is the result of an action, for example a drum stick makes the sound if a drum is hit;

- sound is due to the features or properties of an object; for example it is the rubber in an elastic band that makes the sound.

And here are some further misconceptions that may become apparent as children learn more about the topic:

- sound does not travel outward from a single direction from its source;

- sound does not pass through an object or obstacle;

- muffling a sound makes a sound wave slow down;

- the outer ear is not part of hearing;
- air somehow physically carries sound;
- the making of sound is not linked to vibrations.

Topics and teaching strategies

Sound through the senses

In the new curriculum (DfE, 2013) sound is not directly mentioned at Key Stage 1, but it could be covered when investigating the senses. It suggests pupils should be able to

> *identify, name, draw and label the basic parts of the human body and say which part of the body is associated with each sense.*

(DfE, 2013, page 149)

In order to develop children's awareness of sound at an early age you could ask them to listen to and identify different sounds from their immediate environment. Through recognising and classifying these sounds (*working scientifically*) children will be able to go on to classify or group them into sounds found in different aspects of their lives, such as kitchen sounds (a saucepan), emergency sounds (sirens) and animal sounds (a cow mooing). This can also be extended to grouping sounds into man-made and natural categories. You can at this early age start to get children to think of sounds in terms of soft and loud noises. Through careful observations (*working scientifically*) and discussions you can also help children to draw links between the sense of sound and the organ they have for hearing, ie their ears.

FACTFILE

The outer ear gathers sounds and focuses it to our ears. The ear canal is a tube that runs from the outer to the inner ear. The eardrum is a thin, cone-shaped piece of skin, around 10mm wide. It is positioned between the ear canal and the middle ear. The middle ear is connected to the throat via the Eustachian tube. The inner ear may be thought of in terms of two organs: this includes the semi-circular canals which serve to control the body's balance and the cochlea which changes sound in the form of pressure from the outer ear into electrical impulses which then go to the brain to register the sound (see Figure 11.1).

Children at this early age will not be able to understand fully how the ear works; however, you should encourage them to consider that the outer ear shape is there to collect sounds and that this in turn focuses the sound into the ear ready for it to be identified by the brain.

You could get children, using a mirror, to examine their own ears and then ask them to draw a picture of what they see. Ask them to draw a face diagram with items such as ears and eyes on it and then begin to assess whether they can label the sensory organs.

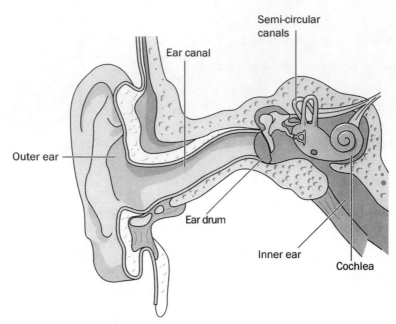

Figure 11.1 *Structure of the human ear*

Sound sources

It is important that young children start to realise that the sounds in the world continue to exist and are created, even if children cannot hear them. To help children consider this idea, ask them if they think sounds are being created in other countries or towns while you are talking. Get them to consider that while they are at school perhaps a friend may be making a noise in the playground and even though it may not have been heard by them that does not mean that others are not hearing it. You can test this idea by making a tape recording of sounds in the environment when children are in lessons and then take these recordings back to the class to listen to.

Similarly, children often feel that sounds can only be heard if they are actively listening to them. But in fact we can hear things even if we are not listening. Perhaps you could ask a child from another class to bang a small drum outside the children's classroom while they are working, starting the banging softly and then increasing its volume so that there can be no doubt it can be heard. This way you can explain to the pupils that they heard the sound even though they were not expecting it.

What is the origin of sound?

It is in Year 4 that the new curriculum suggests that pupils should be taught to:

- *identify how sounds are made, associating some of them with something vibrating;*

- *recognise that vibrations from sounds travel through a medium to the ear.*

(DfE, 2013, page 163)

Young children find it very hard to understand the concept of sound and may even represent the idea of a sound visually with lines in their drawings. More knowledgeable or gifted children may even represent sound in their drawings in terms of a wavy image, this idea being associated with the sound displayed on a monitor. Children also often tend to think that sounds travels as a fast-moving invisible force which does not necessarily need something like air or water to carry it. Some pupils will even think that sound is the result of an action, for example drum sticks hitting a drum, or that the sound is linked to a quality of the material from which an item is made, such as the rubber in a rubber band.

FACTFILE

In order that a sound can be heard it needs to travel through a medium which can be either a solid, liquid or a gas. Sound travels at 6,000m/s through solids such as steel, while in a liquid like water it will travel at 1,500m/s and in a gas such as air, at just 330m/s.

A sound wave or longitudinal wave is introduced into a medium by a vibrating object. The vibrating object is the source of the disturbance that moves through the medium. In a longitudinal wave the molecules move in the same direction as the source of the initial disturbance. Simply put, if the source of the initial vibration comes from the left then the displacement of the molecules will move from the left.

Since the transmission of sound is not easily observed by pupils you can help children conceptualise this idea through the following simple experiment. Use a 'slinky' spring to show how a wave can travel through a substance. Get children to stretch out the slinky spring between their two hands and tell them to give one end a small flick or push, as shown in Figure 11.2. They will be able to see a wave travel along the length of the spring and even bounce along the spring once it has reached the other end.

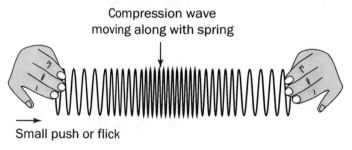

Compression wave
moving along with spring

Small push or flick

Figure 11.2 *Using a slinky to model sound wave transmission*

By encouraging pupils to make close observations (*working scientifically*) during this experiment they will witness the spring being compressed during the wave's movement along the spring. Later you can explain to children that sound waves are longitudinal waves and that sound travels in a similar way to what they have witnessed during this experiment. The source of sound, ie a vibration (what the pupils have now produced in this experiment by giving the spring a flick or push), makes molecules in the air or other mediums pass the sound on as they move back and forth, bouncing off each other, in the same direction as with the wave they observed. You could liken this concept to a wave machine in their local leisure pool in order to further help children conceptualise this idea.

Seeing vibrations that cause sound

To help children see the vibrations that cause sound you can undertake several practical activities.

Firstly you can get them to place a drum on a flat surface and to put some rice grains or sand grains on its surface. Ask them to strike it gently and they will witness these grains bouncing up and down because the drum head or skin is moving up and down very quickly. If they then try striking the drum skin without grains while looking horizontally across it they will see it appear to become fuzzy. This is in fact the drum skin vibrating very quickly and this is caused by them hitting the skin and making it vibrate.

Children can examine plucked guitar strings and see and feel them vibrate. Ask them which string makes the highest or lowest note and how this relates to the speed at which the string vibrates.

Get the children to strike a tuning fork on a soft surface while holding it between their index finger and thumb. Then ask pupils to place one prong gently into a shallow tray of water. Children will quickly notice ripples being created in the water as the vibrations from the tuning fork are transferred. You could also ask the children to place the tuning fork prong on to the underside of a small dish covered in sand. The vibrations from the tuning fork will be transferred through the dish making the sand appear to dance. Alternatively, you could ask pupils to strike a tuning fork and then place it next to a suspended ping-pong ball and watch what happens.

All these experiments will help children to further develop their idea of the role that vibrations play in the creation of sound.

The role of a medium in sound

Often children fail to understand how sounds arrive at the ear and may think that particular packages of air carry the sound to the ear. Therefore it is important that you help children understand that sound is transmitted to their ears through a medium such as air. In order to develop this idea you could try any of the following experiments.

Ask children to create string telephones, by using yoghurt pots or plastic cups. Tell the children to pierce a hole in the bottom of two cups and then thread a 3m piece of string through both holes to connect the cups together. Finally, knot the string at both ends to stop it coming back out of the cup. Ask two children to pull the string taut using the cups and then tell one to whisper HELLO into a cup while the other child listens through the cup at the other end, as shown in Figure 11.3. Then ask the children to whisper to one another from the same distance without the cups. This experiment will allow the children to compare air to string as a medium for carrying sound. By asking the children to firstly predict and then investigate

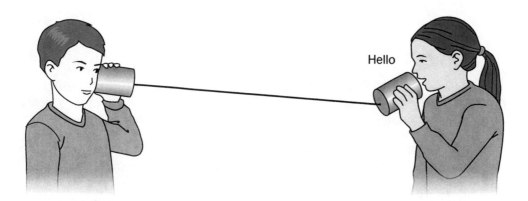

Figure 11.3 *String telephone*

what happens if they cross strings with one another as they speak and listen you will be able to quickly assess how well pupils really understand the concept that sound is carried via a medium. You can also extend this investigation for the more able by asking them to vary the length and type of string used as well as the size and material of the cups used.

Get pupils to listen to a tuning fork close to their ears and then at arm's length in order to further help children explore how well air carries sound. Encourage the children to compare the sounds they hear at both distances and to think whether they feel air is in fact a good medium to transmit sound or not.

Ask a child to place a vibrating tuning fork on to one end of a table while another child has his ear flat on the table at its other end. This way the child will be able to compare whether the tuning fork could be more easily heard through the solid of the table or the air. By carrying out this investigation you will be able to help reinforce the notion that a solid is a much better medium to carry sound than air.

By asking children to draw what they think is happening in these experiments you will be able to assess their understanding of what is going on in terms of sound vibrations travelling through a medium.

Children, given these practical activities, will quickly realise that air is a rather poor medium for transmitting sound compared to solid objects. You can then ask the children to consider and investigate how a liquid compares as a medium to carry sound. Through practical investigations and recording of results (*working scientifically*) you can demonstrate that a liquid such as water is better than air, but less effective than wood as a medium for carrying sound. Perhaps you could suggest that next time the children are swimming they make sounds underwater such as banging wooden blocks together to see if they are audible.

The loudness of sound

The new curriculum suggests pupils in Year 4 should be taught to:

- *find patterns between the volume of a sound and the strength of the vibrations that produced it;*

- *recognise that sounds get fainter as the distance from the sound source increases.*

(DfE, 2013, page 163)

Before you start getting children to understand the concept of volume they must first realise that sounds do get fainter the further away the person listening to them is from the source of that sound, unless of course you increase the volume of that sound.

In order to investigate this phenomenon, ask one child to ring a bell while they are outside while another moves further away from it using predetermined incremental movements.

FACTFILE

The amplitude (loudness) of a sound is determined by the height of the wave. Louder sounds have higher waves. As the amount of energy carried by the wave increases, its amplitude also increases.

Decibels (dB) are the standard units used to measure the loudness of sound.

You can help children start to understand the links between the intensity of energy involved when creating sound and its loudness or volume by asking children to use a range of musical instruments. What happens if they strike, or pluck an instrument softly or with more force? Is the sound louder or softer? You can also, as with previous investigations, use materials such as rice on a drum to show the change in the violence of vibrations by how high the rice flies up from the drum. This way children will quickly learn that the more energy you put into creating the vibration the greater the vibration and hence the louder the sound that is created. You can get pupils to physically model the transmission of different strength vibrations using the following technique. Ask the children to stand one behind each other at arm's length with their tips of their fingers resting on the shoulder of the person in front of them, as shown in Figure 11.4.

Tell the person at the front of the line to make a quiet noise if they feel a gentle push and a louder noise if they feel a harder push. Then ask the child at the back of the line to sensibly start a 'push wave' by gently or more violently pushing on the back of the person in front of them. As each person feels the push they too should push with equal strength on the back of the person in front of them. By doing this the child at the front of the line will make a quiet or louder noise as a result of the push they have felt. By using this technique all the children should be able to start to build a conceptual link between the strength of a push, or in a sound's case its vibration, and its loudness.

While you are teaching children about the concept of loudness it is important that you raise the increasing problem of noise pollution in our daily lives. Encourage children to think of ways of insulating or soundproofing objects since it is not often practical to reduce the loudness of some machines. This will allow you to get children to produce some fair tests to develop the notion of insulating against sound (*working scientifically*) as well as promoting

Figure 11.4 Creating a push wave

an understanding of the need for humans to reduce sound levels while at work, such as on a building site.

For some children the answer to sound reduction and insulation may seem obvious since they carry the misconception that if a room is effectively sealed then sounds will not be able to get in or out through the gaps. Sounds do not easily get through glazed windows because some of the energy is either reflected or absorbed by the glass. But large amounts of the sound's energy will actually make it through the glass and sound is not slowed down as commonly thought. Since sound can permeate materials, how might you reduce or remove the energy from sound waves in order to soundproof a room or object? You can investigate this by getting children to explore (*working scientifically*) what materials or how many layers of materials can stop an electronic alarm from being heard. Through the use of data loggers children can record their results and display them in the form of a bar graph in order to draw conclusions about which materials are best for soundproofing.

Pitch and frequency

The new curriculum suggests pupils in Year 4 should be taught to

> find patterns between the pitch of a sound and the features of the object that produced it.

(DfE, 2013, page 163)

Now that children are getting more confident with the concepts and vocabulary of sound and have created many sounds of their own it is important that they understand what causes a sound to be high or low.

FACTFILE

When a sound wave is created the molecules in a medium through which the sound is travelling will move in a back and forth motion at a given frequency. The frequency of a wave refers to how often the molecules in the medium vibrate when a wave passes through any medium. The frequency of a wave is measured by the number of complete back and forth vibrations of a molecule of the medium in a fixed unit of time.

Hertz (Hz) are used to measure a particular frequency that is responsible for a particular note. The lowest frequency that can be detected by a human is approximately 20Hz while the highest frequency is around 20,000Hz.

The pitch of a sound is how high or low the sound or note appears. Though sound waves themselves do not have pitch, sound waves' back and forward motion can be measured in order to obtain a frequency. High-pitched notes have a higher frequency which may be seen on a stringed instrument, as the faster vibrations of a string will cause high-pitch notes, and low-pitched notes will have a lower frequency which can be seen in terms of a lower speed of vibrating strings.

Once children are confident with the notion of vibrations causing sound you can then move on to consider the concepts of the pitch of a note and its frequency. If children have started to notice the back and forth motion of a vibration you can introduce the idea of frequency and the concept that the faster the frequency the higher the note. Several investigations can aid understanding of this idea, with one example as follows.

Provide children with sturdy trays or boxes and two different sorts of elastic band. Pupils should only just be able to stretch one elastic band over the tray, while the other should be relatively loose once stretched into place in order to create a simple guitar, as shown in Figure 11.5. Ask the children to pluck both bands and note what happens to the bands' movement and, as a consequence of this, the vibrations that are caused. The children will see that the tighter elastic band vibrates faster than the loosely stretched one.

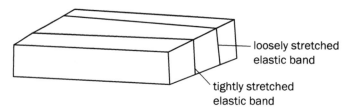

Figure 11.5 *A simple guitar using elastic bands*

By getting children to concentrate on the pitch of the sound, as well as the number of vibrations observed, they will start to make a valuable link between the pitch of a note and the frequency with which an object vibrates.

Changing pitch using blowing

You can also investigate how differing pitches are created in wind-blown instruments; such instruments can be found within the woodwind section of the orchestra.

Ask pupils to blow over the rim of a plastic or glass bottle such as a milk bottle and listen to the sounds that are produced. If the children hold the bottles they will also be able to feel the vibrations that are being created as they blow across the bottle's rim. You can ask children to fill the bottle with different amounts of water and then ask them to predict (*working scientifically*) if more or less water in the bottle will create a higher or lower pitched note.

Ask the children to try and explain why blowing across the bottle rim makes a particular sound, to see if they understand how vibrations produce a particular pitch of note.

Children should realise that it is the air in the bottle that is vibrating or resonating and that the smaller the volume of air in the bottle the higher the pitch that is created and can be heard. You can then ask children to start to consider how musicians playing woodwind instruments control the pitch of their instruments by altering the length of the vibrating column of air in the instrument.

Echoes

Though the new curriculum (DfE, 2013) does not require children to investigate the creation and causes of echoes you should encourage children to study this aspect of sound while generally studying this topic, not only because it allows for a child's deeper conceptual understanding of this topic, but also because it helps them to further understand how sounds are formed and used on our planet.

By getting children to investigate how sound vibrations are reflected off different types of surfaces pupils will soon realise that hard and smooth surfaces are the most conducive to creating echoes. Children should be encouraged to think of their own homes and how soft furnishings reduce echoes while an empty room increases them.

This study of the property of sounds can be extended to consider how items such as ear trumpets, like the outer ear, may be used to help gather and collect sounds so that they can be more easily heard if they are, for example, quiet or distant. You can also ask children to consider the collection of sound waves on a bigger scale by the use of parabolic dishes.

You can extend children's understanding of the reflective nature and properties of sound by thinking of animals such as bats and dolphins. By giving out high-frequency sounds which are reflected off surfaces these animals use sound reflections to navigate and to locate their food sources. Some animals use their large ears to collect and gather the sounds around them in order to stay safe from predators.

This study of sound will allow you to investigate with children how we have adapted the skills developed by animals and used our developing knowledge of sound to benefit humans through the development of sonar and ultrasound.

CROSS-CURRICULAR LINKS

Literacy

Literacy can be promoted through a variety of means. You can encourage children to listen to the rhymes and rhythms of poems such as *Night Mail* by WH Auden or Wes Magee's *Boneyard Rap* in order for children to understand how sound can be used in poems to create effect.

You can also encourage pupils to develop their listening and oral skills through the use of debates. Children can write their own plays and devise sound effects, such as those used in programmes such as *The Archers* to bring the written word to life.

Numeracy

Numeracy can be promoted by looking at the scales that record audible sound. You can also look into the use of sound as a means of delivering code, such as Morse.

Other curricular links

Sounds may also be examined through the wider topic of communication. You could focus on an historical study into how early writing has been superseded by the advent of telephone, radio and television, or also historically how the work of individuals in the Second World War who worked for the government at places such as Bletchley Park deciphered sound codes to gain an advantage over our enemies. You can explore the modern concept of noise pollution and examine how an airport's geographical location may cause issues for residents. Other sources of sounds such as foghorns can lead to an understanding of our maritime history, with animal sounds such as rattlesnakes enabling you to explore the habitats and environments of other countries. Music will inevitably allow you to explore the world of sound through instruments of the orchestra. You will also be able to make geographical links to the variety of instruments that can be found around the world and the types of instruments that are played. Composers such as Beethoven (who eventually went deaf) will provide an opportunity for you to explore how disabilities may be overcome in order for individuals to succeed in things that they desire to do. If you wish to consider this issue from a more contemporary musician, Dame Evelyn Glennie provides an excellent example.

HEALTH AND SAFETY

Remember to warn children of the dangers of:

- poking anything into their ears;
- shouting loudly into someone's ear or shouting/blowing if someone is listening through a sound tube;
- shared mouthpieces (these should be sterilised before each use).

Critical questions

» *On a scale of 1–10 (with 10 being completely confident) how confident do you now feel in your own subject knowledge of sound as a topic?*

» *Identify the specific areas where you feel less confident.*

» *Where else might you look and what else might you do to develop your subject knowledge in those areas?*

» *What resources do you need to collect in order to successfully start teaching this topic?*

» *Where might you take pupils in order to develop their subject knowledge? Are there any good science-based exploratory centres you can visit to help children experience bigger equipment such as parabolic dishes?*

Taking it further

Books

ASE (2014) *Be Safe in Science*, 4th Edition. Hatfield: ASE.

Burne, D (1991) *How Nature Works*. London: Dorling and Kindersley.

Wenham, M and Ovens, P (2010) *Understanding Primary Science*, 3rd Edition. London: Sage Publications.

Early Years rhymes such as *Old MacDonald Had a Farm* can be found in, for example: Wingate, P (Ed.) (2008) *The Nursery Rhyme Book: Remember the Rhymes of Yesterday*. London: Micheal O'Mara Books.

Websites

www.kidsplanet.org/games/js/whoami.html (accessed 5 February 2014).

www.primaryhomeworkhelp.co.uk/revision/Science/sounds.html (accessed 5 February 2014).

British Library Sound archive available at http://sounds.bl.uk/ (accessed 5 February 2014).

References

DfE (2013) *Teachers' Standards*. www.gov.uk/government/uploads/system/uploads/attachment_data/file/208682/Teachers__Standards_2013.pdf (accessed 17 February 2014).

12 Electricity

Introduction

Electricity is an essential part of modern living. It makes things around us work, provides lighting and heating and serves as a source of energy for many of the appliances we use and take for granted in our everyday life. Children become aware of electricity very early on and should always be reminded of the dangers associated with it. It is useful to stress that the equipment children use in school is safe, due to its low voltage and will not involve mains electricity. It is conceptually complex. We can for example see the effects of electricity but we often cannot understand what is happening. Analogies, for example a water pump and an electric circuit, can be very effective in helping children to understand some of these difficult concepts, and children should be given the opportunity to learn about electricity through exploration, discussion and application. Electricity in the new national curriculum is more about children doing, rather than understanding and being able to explain what is happening. It is now required to be taught only at Key Stage 2 and not at Key Stage 1.

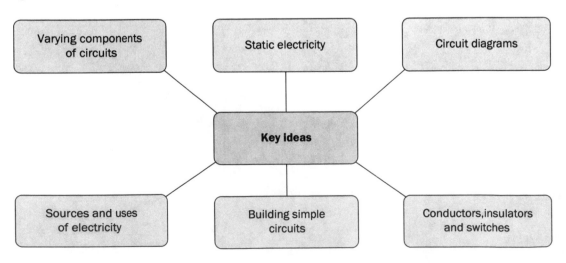

KEY VOCABULARY

The new national curriculum (DfE, 2013) stresses the importance of children using technical terminology accurately and precisely and building up an extended specialist vocabulary. It is also necessary for pupils to understand the context in which the scientific vocabulary is used. In Year 4 pupils should become familiar with the names of common electrical components such as **cell**, **battery**, **wire**, **lamp**, **filament**, **switches**, **buzzers** and **motors**. They should use terms such as **circuit**, **series circuit** and work with **conductors** and **insulators**. In Year 4 they might use the terms **current** and **voltage** but these should not be introduced formally until Year 6.

CHILDREN'S IDEAS AND COMMON MISCONCEPTIONS

Children have many misconceptions about what electricity is and how it works. Young children may think that:

* electricity is a kind of material contained in the battery;

* it is a material which goes to a bulb;

* energy is used up by the bulb;

* the distance of the bulb from the battery will determine how brightly it shines;

* only one wire is needed to light a bulb as household appliances are connected to the mains by a single wire;

* the current moves along both wires and clashes in the middle causing the bulb to light;

* two wires need to be attached to the battery, but do not connect the wires to the correct places on the bulb, or the terminals on the battery.

As children get older and start building circuit diagrams with more than one component they may think that:

* when circuits have two bulbs in series, the first bulb will be brighter than the second bulb, as the first wire will have used up some of the electricity that is going round, so there will be less for the second bulb;

* the flow of current is less in the return wire;

* the current is not the same in all parts of the circuit and gets used up.

FACTFILE

The term 'lamp' is the name for the whole lighting component. The bulb is only the glass part. Most batteries are chemical cells. A chemical cell converts chemical energy into electrical energy.

Topics and teaching strategies

Sources and uses of electricity

The new curriculum suggests pupils in Year 4 should be taught to

> *identify common appliances that use electricity.*
>
> (DfE, 2013, page 164)

FACTFILE

Electricity is a type of energy which provides power to make things work, such as a hair dryer. It can be converted into other forms of energy, eg heat, light, sound and movement (kinetic energy).

An electric current is the movement of charged particles (electrons) through a conductor. A conductor is a material which allows this flow of electrons to take place.

An effective way of starting the topic of electricity is to ask pupils what they have in their homes that works with electricity so they can relate it to their own experiences, or get them to list the different ways in which we use electricity. You might ask pupils to bring in toys that have an electrical component, eg a light, motor or alarm. You could show children some electrical appliances and talk about the need to use the appliance safely for its intended purpose. This could lead to a discussion of what they should not do around electrical items, including putting objects into sockets, sticking a knife in a toaster while it is on, taking appliances apart, putting the appliance in water or touching a switch with wet hands. Children with special needs or with English as an additional language could access the same knowledge and understanding if you provide them with a picture showing some of the dangers of electricity and ask them to circle the dangers.

Building simple circuits

FACTFILE

Electricity travels in a circle from the battery, back to the battery via a device such as a bulb which works when electricity goes through it (see Figure 12.1). A battery is made of a mixture

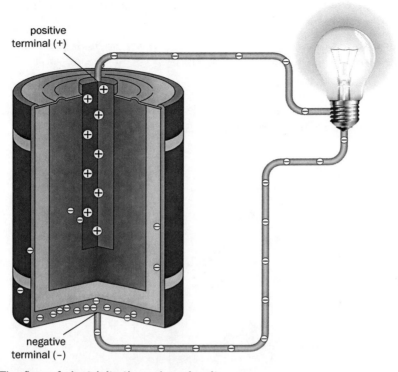

positive
terminal (+)

negative
terminal (−)

Figure 12.1 *The flow of electricity through a circuit*

of chemicals which react together to produce a surplus of electrons at the negative terminal of the battery and a shortage of electrons on the positive terminal. When a conductor such as a metal wire links the negative terminal with the positive terminal, all the electrons in the wire immediately start to move away from the negative charge at one terminal and are attracted towards the positive charge at the other terminal. This causes movement of electrons through the wire and an electric current flows. There is no bunching up of electrons anywhere in the circuit. The rate of movement of electrons through the wire is called a current and is measured in amps (A). Using an ammeter to measure the flow of electricity in a series circuit will show that it is the same at any point.

The correct term for a single battery is a cell. 4.5v batteries are the most commonly used in schools. An electric current has three main parts:

1.   the power supply (cell);

2.   the conductor (wire) which carries the current;

3.   the load (electrical device such as a lamp, motor or buzzer).

Once children have an appreciation of the sources, uses and dangers of electricity they can progress to working with simple circuits. The new curriculum suggests that pupils in Year 4 should be taught to:

- *construct a simple series electrical circuit, identifying and naming its basic parts, including cells, wires, bulbs, switches and buzzers;*

- *identify whether or not a lamp will light in a simple series circuit, based on whether or not the lamp is part of a complete loop with a battery.*

(DfE, 2013, page 164)

An excellent activity to carry out with children is to ask them to light a lamp using only one cell, one lamp and one wire, as seen in Figure 12.2.

Figure 12.2 *Simple circuit using one cell, one lamp and one wire*

Encourage the children to problem solve with the equipment provided, for example they should consider which part of the cell touches which part of the bulb and how they think the bulb works. Sometimes children find it difficult to attach the wire to the correct part of the bulb and cell so use adhesive tape to help keep the wire in place at this point. It is important that children carry out this activity without using bulb holders and battery holders so they can appreciate which parts of the wire need to touch which parts of the cell (battery) and bulb, and that a completed circuit is required for the bulb to light. Using wires rather than crocodile clips also helps them to see and understand that the end of the wire needs to have the metal inside it exposed (the conductor) and touch the metal end of the cell.

FACTFILE

Electricity will travel through all components in a circuit including inside the bulb. In a bulb the electricity passes through a very thin wire called the filament, usually made of the metal tungsten. The electrons need to squeeze through this very thin wire and as they do, they collide much more frequently with the atoms of the metal. This transfers energy to the wire making the atoms vibrate much faster. This causes the filament to get very hot. Tungsten has a very high melting point so instead of melting, the filament becomes white hot. The glow from this heat is seen as light. The glass surround protects the fine wire and is filled by an inert gas called argon that will not react with it. It is important to note that no electrons are used up in lighting a bulb. The moving electrons (the current) are the means by which energy is transferred to the bulb from the battery. Therefore, it is the energy which is transferred to the bulb, not the electrons or current.

Inside a lamp

An interesting activity to follow this is to provide the children with magnifying glasses and ask them to draw what is inside the lamp (see Factfile above), as seen in Figure 12.3. This will help them comprehend how electricity flows inside the bulb and the function of the different parts.

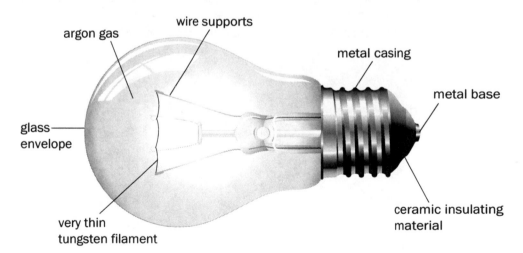

Figure 12.3 *Inside a lamp*

A series circuit is a circuit where all components are connected end-to-end to form only one path for electrons to flow through the circuit. Pupils can construct simple series circuits using a bulb, cell and two wires, as in Figure 12.4. Ask the children to record their work in the form of pictures or use a digital camera and take photographs and explain what is happening. Prompt them to identify the purposes of different components.

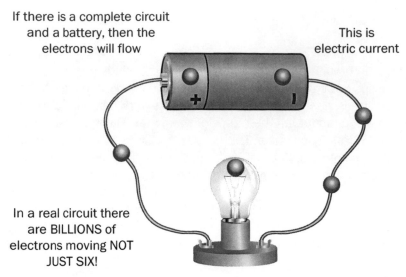

If there is a complete circuit
and a battery, then the
electrons will flow

This is
electric current

In a real circuit there
are BILLIONS of
electrons moving NOT
JUST SIX!

Figure 12.4 *Simple circuit with cell, lamp and two wires*

Building circuits using different components

Children can experiment by substituting the lamp with different components such as a motor or a buzzer. Ask your pupils to explore what happens when they pass electricity through the motor with a propeller attached. Then prompt them to change the wires over at the terminals of the cell (ie attach the wire that was on the positive terminal to the negative terminal and vice versa). They should notice that the direction of the propeller changes from clockwise to anti-clockwise.

FACTFILE

Inside a motor is a coil of wire mounted between two magnets. When the current in the coil is turned on, the coil behaves like a magnet and moves. The current in the coil needs to be reversed every half turn, known as an alternating current, to keep a motor rotating in the same direction. When the wires are swapped at the terminals of the battery, it causes a reverse in the direction of the magnetic field around it and this gives rise to the motor moving in the other direction.

Another activity to try is to ask the pupils to explore what happens when they pass electricity through a buzzer. They should discover that when the red wire in the buzzer is attached to the positive terminal of the cell and the black wire to the negative terminal, the buzzer will work. If the red wire is attached to the negative terminal and the black wire is attached to the positive terminal, the buzzer will not work.

Switches, conductors and insulators

The new curriculum states that pupils in Year 4 should be taught to:

-   *recognise that a switch opens and closes a circuit and associate this with whether or not a lamp lights in a simple series circuit;*

- *recognise some common conductors and insulators, and associate metals with being good conductors.*

(DfE, 2013, page 164)

FACTFILE

A completed circuit is needed for a device such as a lamp to work. Where there is a break in the circuit, for example an open switch, the lamp will not light.

Provide the children with a selection of switches and ask them to incorporate them into the circuits and discuss with each other how they work. Provide them with some equipment and ask them to make their own switches such as the ones shown in Figure 12.5 using a paperclip, two drawing pins and some card or wood to attach the drawing pins and paperclip to. The clip is bent so that it does not touch the drawing pin on the right unless it is pressed.

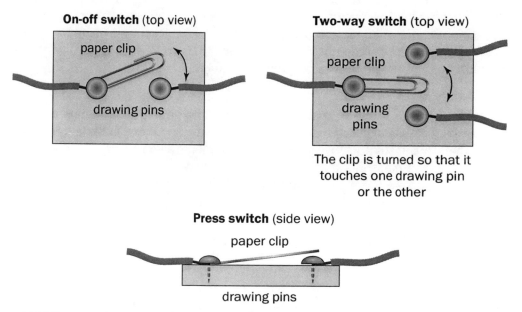

Figure 12.5 One-way, two-way and press switches

An exciting activity to carry out with your more able pupils is to ask them to make a switch and incorporate it into a circuit with a bulb which would be suitable to send Morse code signals, a method of transmitting information using light.

Another way of extending your more able pupils and illustrating the role of the switch in breaking or completing a circuit and allowing the flow of electricity, is through the use of the ball analogy. Gather children in a circle, give each child a ball and say the ball is an electron. Ask each child to pass their ball or electron to the person on their right. The person on the right receives the ball from their left and passes it to the person on their right and so on. There is one child who has a hat on who is the switch. The movement of the balls is the current. When the child acting as the switch says off and turns 90 degrees, all the balls stop moving simultaneously because the switch is open and the flow or current is interrupted.

Some materials are good conductors of electricity and allow the flow of electrons. Some materials will not allow the flow of electrons and are known as insulators.

FACTFILE

All materials are made up of small particles called atoms. The nucleus of an atom is made up of neutrons which have no charge, and protons which are positively charged. Electrons circle the nucleus of the atom and have a negative charge and are repelled by other electrons. In metals the outermost electrons are not bound tightly to the centre of the atom and are free to move around the atoms. In non-metals electrons are much more tightly bound to individual atoms, these materials are often insulators. If the material allows the movement of electrons it is called a conductor. The thickness of the conductor affects the ability of the electrons to move, ie a thinner wire will have greater resistance than a thicker wire made from the same material. Metals contain a large number of electrons that are free to move so relatively little push, ie a low voltage will produce a current in these materials.

Provide children with a range of materials such as different types of metals, card, paper, rubber or pencil graphite and ask them to investigate which of these materials conduct electricity and which are insulators. They could sort them into two groups and look for similar characteristics in the materials that conduct electricity (*working scientifically*). This activity will help them associate metals with being good conductors. The pencil graphite will challenge your more able pupils as it will conduct electricity.

Varying components in a circuit

By the time pupils are in Year 6 they should build on the work done in Year 4 and be able to answer questions about what happens when they use different components within a circuit, eg switches, bulbs, buzzers and motors. They could investigate whether bulbs get brighter if more bulbs are added, or if the bulb gets brighter if more cells are added. They could observe the effect of changing one component at a time in a circuit. It is vital that the necessary precautions for working safely with electricity are also reiterated before starting the topic in Year 6. The new national curriculum states that when pupils are in Year 6 they should be able to:

- *associate the brightness of a lamp or the volume of a buzzer with the number and voltage of cells used in the circuit;*

- *compare and give reasons for variations in how components function, including the brightness of bulbs, the loudness of buzzers and the on/off position of switches.*

(DfE, 2013, page 175)

FACTFILE

Bulbs can be made brighter or dimmer in a circuit by varying the number of cells, or varying the resistance of the circuit. This can be done by changing the number of bulbs or type of bulb. The greater the surplus of electrons at one terminal of the battery, and the greater the deficit of electrons at the other terminal, the greater the push of the battery. The strength of its pushing power is called the potential difference and is measured in volts. Cells and batteries have a certain voltage rating. The rate of movement of electrons through the wire is called current and is measured in amps. Resistance tells us something about the amount of voltage needed to send a particular current through a component. Resistance is measured in OHMS. All components, eg bulbs and motors, have resistance, some more than others. $V = I \times R$ where V is the voltage, I is the current and R is the resistance.

The water pump is a well-known analogy used to describe an electric current. The amount of water flowing around all parts of the pipe is the same. The pump gives the power or energy and makes the water wheel turn just like the battery produces the current which makes the bulb light up. Be aware that when using this analogy, children might think that if the pipe breaks the electrons will flow out. This is one of the disadvantages of this analogy.

A powerful way of helping children understand that the brightness of a lamp depends on the voltage of the cells used in the circuit and the resistance in the circuit is by using the string analogy. Ask the children to support a complete circle of string by holding the string very loosely between their thumb and first finger. The string represents the wire. You can act as the battery and cause the string to move by pulling it gently. The moving string is the current and it moves simultaneously in all parts of the circuit. The same amount of string leaves the battery as returns to it. You can also have one child acting as a bulb and holding the string more tightly or resisting the flow. Eventually the battery starts to run down and you correspond by becoming tired and pulling the string more slowly. Eventually when the battery has run down the string will stop moving around. A battery becomes flat when it can no longer push the electrons. Alternatively, add two batteries to the circuit by having the teacher and another pupil being the batteries and move the string faster around the circuit because there is double the power there to move the electrons around. More able children could be given the task to debate the advantages and disadvantages of the string analogy.

Children might be posed a problem and asked to design and make a lighthouse with a series circuit and switch which will light up a bulb, or design a burglar alarm which includes a circuit.

Circuit diagrams

The new national curriculum states that when pupils are in Year 6 they should be able to

use recognised symbols when representing a simple circuit diagram.

(DfE, 2013, page 175)

Children in Year 4 will have recorded their circuit diagrams in the form of pictures rather than circuit diagrams using the correct symbols for the different electrical components. In Year 6 they will be required to represent their circuit diagrams using the standard symbols shown in Figure 12.6. A child's record of a circuit with a switch, a cell and a lamp should thus look like the one in Figure 12.7. Note that all components are linked and that there are no gaps except with the switch which is open.

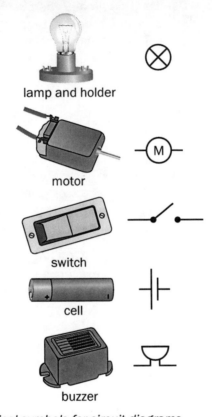

lamp and holder

motor

switch

cell

buzzer

Figure 12.6 *Standard electrical symbols for circuit diagrams*

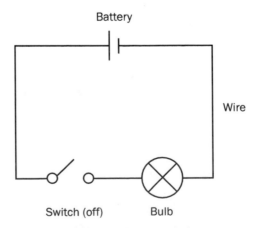

Figure 12.7 *Simple circuit diagram using standard symbols*

Static electricity

Children may ask you about the electricity in lightning or the crackle when they brush their hair which may result in you teaching aspects of static electricity, although static electricity is not part of the new national curriculum.

FACTFILE

The surface of some materials, eg non-metallic ones, can be electrically charged by rubbing with another material. In this instance the electrons held by atoms are removed from the surfaces of these substances. Rubbing a balloon against a woolly jumper will cause electrons to move from the surface of your jumper to spread out on the surface of the balloon. This gives the balloon an excess of electrons and therefore a negative charge. If the balloon is placed near a wall which has a positive charge, the balloon will stick to the wall as negative and positive charges attract each other. This electricity is referred to as static because the charge does not flow in the materials but remains on the surface. In the atmosphere, water droplets collide with each other and become negatively charged. Static electricity causes lightning as this build-up of negative charge is discharged down to Earth as light. This static electricity can produce high voltages.

Try the above activity with the balloon with the children or ask them to think about when they encounter static electricity in their daily lives. Reinforce the safety aspects of electricity by talking to the children about the dangers of flying a kite near electricity pylons.

CROSS-CURRICULAR LINKS

Literacy

Children can pretend to be newspaper reporters and interview Volta who created the first electric battery. They could report the invention of Michael Faraday as a newspaper article in a national newspaper. They could use the internet and research and make some notes into how Morse code has been used in the past.

Numeracy

In mathematics children could be shown how electricity is measured. They could think of different ways of sorting materials into conductors and insulators using, for example, Venn diagrams or Carroll diagrams.

Other curriculum areas

In design and technology they could design and make a lighthouse with a bulb that lights and a switch that can be used to switch the lighthouse on or off. Alternatively, they could make an electrical-powered buggy using a motor and a battery. In art they could design a poster which illustrates the dangers of electricity and warn other children. As part of their history, they could learn about the discovery of electricity by the ancient Greeks. In geography they could find out about different ways in which electricity is produced and develop their knowledge and understanding of renewable and non-renewable resources.

HEALTH AND SAFETY

Be Safe in Science (ASE, 2010) provides some useful information on things to take into consideration when teaching this topic and is a good source of reference, along with the following:

- mains electricity is much more powerful than electricity from batteries;

- do not open or cut up batteries as the chemicals inside are dangerous;

- do not use rechargeable batteries as they can cause short circuits;

- if the ends of rechargeable batteries and alkali batteries are connected with a wire or a metal object, ie short circuited, these can become hot enough to cause minor burns;

- if you connect a 1.5v lamp to a 4.5v battery, it will become very hot;

- any electrical devices used in schools need to be checked for electrical safety by a qualified person;

- do not conduct electrical experiments near any source of water and ensure all hands are dry.

Critical questions

» *On a scale of 1–10 (with 10 being completely confident) how confident do you now feel in your own subject knowledge of electricity as a topic?*

» *Where else might you look and what else might you do to develop your subject knowledge?*

» *What resources do you need to collect in order to successfully start teaching this topic?*

» *Where might you take pupils in order to develop their subject knowledge? Are there any school visits you could do?*

Taking it further

Mant, J, Wilson, H (2007) Understanding Simple Circuits. *Primary Science Review*, May/June.

Russell, T and Watt, D (1990) *Electricity, SPACE Research Report*. Liverpool: Liverpool University Press.

Websites

www.bbc.co.uk/programmes/p00kjq6d

www.gizmoandwidget.com

www.howstuffworks.com/index.htm

http://learningcircuits.co.uk/

www.teachersmedia.co.uk/subjects/primary/electricity-magnetism

References

ASE (2010) *Be Safe in Science*. Hatfield: ASE.

DfE (2013) *Teachers' Standards*. www.gov.uk/government/uploads/system/uploads/attachment_data/file/208682/Teachers__Standards_2013.pdf (accessed 17 February 2014).

Index